EXPOSING
SATAN AND
BINDING HIM UP

EXPOSING
SATAN AND
BINDING HIM UP

BYRON WALKER

TATE PUBLISHING
AND ENTERPRISES, LLC

Published by Tate Publishing & Enterprises, LLC
127 E. Trade Center Terrace | Mustang, Oklahoma 73064 USA
1.888.361.9473 | www.tatepublishing.com

Tate Publishing is committed to excellence in the publishing industry. The company reflects the philosophy established by the founders, based on Psalm 68:11,
"The Lord gave the word and great was the company of those who published it."

Book design copyright © 2013 by Tate Publishing, LLC. All rights reserved.
Cover design by Joel Uber
Interior design by Jomel Pepito

Published in the United States of America

ISBN: 978-1-62510-155-6
1. Religion / General
2. Religion / Christianity / General
13.07.11

DEDICATION

I will greatly like to dedicate this book to my Savior, Deliverer, and Redeemer, the one who is the sustainer of my life, Jesus Christ. For without Jesus and the sweet fragrance of his Spirit, this book would have never come to life. I thank my heavenly Father for using me as a living vessel to proclaim the Gospel to the world.

Truly, I honor you, God, for it's in you that I live, I breath and have my being; for I know that after everything else fails, Lord, your Word will stand. Thank you, Lord, for being my greatest encourager!

ACKNOWLEDGMENTS

I would first like to thank my parents whom I love very dearly for being there for me in the good times as well as the bad, Pamela and Bruce Walker. Mom, you have taught me what it is to serve the Lord, and you have encouraged me to continue in doing the works of the Lord. I thank you for helping me and encouraging me to do my best! I love you dearly! Dad, thank you for the love you have given me throughout the years. Know that I appreciate what you have done and what you continue to do and that you are not forgotten. To my brother Clint Walker, thank you for the times of laughter that we have shared and the times of us hanging out and going to the mall shopping. I enjoy those brother moments. You are very special to me in many ways! I love you, Clint, and I am glad that you are my brother. To my sister Romeika Easter, know that I love you and that you are someone really special in my life, and I am glad to also have you as my sister! Also a shout-out goes to my niece Kadaija and to my nephews Demarjay and Cameron. I love you all!

A special thank-you goes to my beautiful and wonderful grandma, Ms. Gover Lee Pierce. Grandma, I can't leave you out of this because if it wasn't for you, I wouldn't be here today!

I will like to thank all of my other family on both sides; I have so many of you to thank! Charkeitha LaDawn Brown, thank you for being the one who I can talk to anytime. I love you, my wonderful cousin. Know that you are truly blessed, and I am truly blessed to have you in my life! Also, I would love to thank Aunt Shirley White, Aunt Sandra, and Aunt Loretta Strayhand. I love you so very much, and you are truly all great aunties of mine! Aunt Versie, thank you for being there for me whenever I needed you and for always keeping a positive attitude. Cousin Nelda Shavers, keep God first and know that I love you a lot; you are such a blessing, and I am proud to have you as my family. Thank you to my auntie and uncle, Mr. and Mrs. Tony, Vennessa Glenn and family, thank you both for being people I can call on, and you both are good family to have. Also to the rest of the family, I wish you all the best! There was never a time that you all were not there when I called on you!

A special note goes to my godparents David and Stephanie Campbell. Thank you both for being there for me. Godmom, I thank you for being the one who I could talk to during my different phases of life. You are truly special in ways that you probably don't even know about!

To my other godparent Apostle Carolyn Cobbs Brown, thank you for encouraging me to do my best. You were the one that helped me to walk in my calling. You were the one that saw in me what I could not see in myself. I thank God for you and the rest of the family!

To Bruce and Cora Wilson, thank you both for being the ones to stand there and help me with a lot of things. If I haven't met you all, especially you, Cora, I wouldn't probably be finishing up my degree to this day! I am finally doing something that I love because you didn't give up on me! I love both you and your husband; you both mean the world to me!

I would like to send a special shout-out to Eden Christian Center Bishop Anthony and First Lady Tajmina Chavers for such great encouragement! Thank you both for everything. I love you both!

I would like to send a special shout-out to Lawrence Rutherford, Mrs. Laura Keith, Pastor Shane Wall, Pastor Vandarray Jackson Dericho and all of HPAN Ministries, Pastor Larry and First Lady Benson, Elder Rockridge Hannah and the rest of Holy Temple COGIC family, Pastors Gregory and Valerie Rogers, and A Word in Season Church family, thank you all for your love and generous support in my ministry. May God continue to bless you and your ministry! I would like to thank all of those who helped me in many ways possible. You are not missed! Know that the best is yet to come! And that everything that God has promised will come to pass!

A special acknowledgment goes out to my wonderful publishing company Tate Publishing. I want to thank all of those who spent substantial time with me in the editing process of my book. Thank you for giving me the opportunity to share my book with the world. Way to go, Tate Publishing, for all of your hard work that you put into every page of this book!

CONTENTS

INTRODUCTION

When you look at the meaning of the word *expose*, it alone lets you know that something is going to be revealed. The Word of God reveals to us information on Satan and his weapons of mass destruction; however, one of Satan's primary tools that we will find is to keep the church in total ignorance to his many schemes, tricks, and lies. Satan's primary objective is to blind the minds of people from receiving the truth because if a person begins to grab hold of the truth, Satan knows that his plans can no longer work.

As I began to bask in God's presence precisely before writing this book, God revealed to me the major reason why a lot of individuals aren't set free is because of the lack of honesty. If people can just be real with themselves, true deliverance will flow freely into their lives. This is the time that we stop substituting the

Byron Walker

devil's name to make him look good. We must realize that there is a real devil, and he must be exposed!

Are you tired of the same ole', same ole' going to church Sunday after Sunday and not being set free? Are you tired of going to church enjoying the dancing, enjoying the music, and getting your praise on after the preacher has preached a happy message; but when you leave church, you arrive home to a place filled with chaos and confusion?

Let me be real with you for a minute; these individuals who are being targeted by the enemy attend church service on a weekly basis and are preached to the same message: "Turn around three times and tell the devil I'm spinning out of the storm!" And they keep confessing the same line of words over again, but in reality, they find themselves spinning right back into the storm that they came out of. Many are jumping and shouting over the issues of things that need to be addressed. However, something needs to change!

We must come to a place in God where we are not afraid to expose the truth. We cannot disregard any corners when it comes to sin. Now is the time for the church to rise in great victory! The hour has finally come for God's children to regain everything that the enemy has stolen from them in the past! I decree and declare from this day forward you will not undergo anymore lack! I decree and declare that there will be an open door for you to walk in the many blessings of the Lord without any hindrances standing in the way! I decree and declare that you will seize great opportunities without any fear, anxiety, or frustration for this is the season that you walk in your desired dream and vision that God has given you with purpose!

The world is groaning for the truth. The world is in a stage of hunger, desiring for more of God, desiring to have a personal encounter with the Father; however, the world cannot receive the truth if they have never been taught the truth. There is a real devil that is lurking throughout society today, and in order for us to defeat him, the truth has to be told! We cannot continue to go any further professing that everything is all right. It is not all right for people to remain captive in the enemy's chains forever. I highly believe that many are afraid to confront Satan to his face because if they expose him to his face for too long, he might just end up exposing the real them.

God is requiring for his children to walk holy before him. He is requiring that we be committed to ministry, declaring his Word to everyone we meet. There are many people who are searching for something real, and there are far too many counterfeits that are already in the world; and many of these individuals that are searching for the real are not only looking for someone who is going to quote the Word, but someone who is willing to live it. This is day for the real saints of God to rise up and take a stand!

This book should be a guide to help you recognize the enemy, overcome his plots, and unleash the power of God into your everyday life. This book should help you know your dominion, walk in your dominion, and know your rightful place in the kingdom of God. You must now walk in the liberty in which Jesus Christ has set you free! God doesn't want for you to walk around like there are chains holding you bound but to see you walking in total victory. Do you know you have the victory? Now is the time for you to walk in it! For you are a victor and not the devil's victim.

I truly believe that if you are bound reading this book, by the time you are finished, every chain of the enemy will be broken from out of your life. God orchestrated this time for you to proclaim everything that you have been searching for. Your deliverance, freedom, and liberty is now, and so get excited because Jesus came to set your captives free and know this, "Whom the Son sets free are truly free indeed" (John 8:36).

SPIRIT VS. FLESH

For the desire of the flesh are opposed to the [Holy] spirit, and the desires of the spirit are opposed to the flesh (godless human nature); for these are antagonistic to each other [continually withstanding and in conflict with each other]; so that you are not free *but* are prevented from doing what you desire to do.

Galatians 5:17 (AMP)

Children of God we are in a battle. We are battling between two opponents: spirit vs. flesh. One of the questions that many wonder at times is this, "How do I know when I am satisfying the flesh, and how do I know when I am satisfying the spirit?" This is how you will know: The flesh always bends you toward the devil; however, the spirit always draws you closer to God.

Have you ever experienced a time in your life where your flesh really wanted something, but way deep in your most inner being something kept saying, "Turn the other way"? There have been times when I had the desire to do things that I thought were good but were not; unfortunately, because of my own desire and not what God wanted from me, I had to reap the consequence. There are some issues in each one of our lives that we need to die from so that God can elevate us to a higher realm in him. Some things and some people who are in our lives have already been expired, and the reason why some of us find it very difficult to find relief and to move to the next spiritual level is because many of us are carrying outdated things and outdated people that God is telling us to get rid of. You and I cannot receive all that God is willing to give us being in the flesh. The flesh is a monster that doesn't quit nagging about the things that it wants, but when our flesh is craving something that is not in the will of God, it should not be fed; but what we should do is aim at feeding our spirit with the Word of God. Our spirit is craving for more of God, but the flesh just keeps fighting.

In the book of Matthew 4:4 (KJV), Jesus shows us the importance of his word, for he declares, "Man shall not live by bread alone, but by every word that proceedeth out of the mouth of God."

My brothers and my sisters, you must realize that one day, heaven and earth are going to both pass away! But there is one thing that will stand forever even when heaven and earth is all gone; God's word is the only sure foundation that will stand forever (God's word is *yea* and *amen*). We have to stand on the promise of God knowing what he says will surely come to pass. Our spirit has to be fed on the word of God in order to grow, and the more word we feed our spirit, the more power we will receive to defeat the devil and live a life full of success.

In the word you will be able to experience the voice of God and read what his many thoughts are concerning you—for his thoughts are life, peace, and of a good report. If you ever want to know what God is thinking, search the Scriptures, and in them you will find the most fascinating things that you never knew about God before pertaining to you.

SPIRIT VS. FLESH

In this fleshy nature of ours, our stomach knows exactly when it is the right time to eat. When that time comes and we begin to ignore our stomach's urge for food, it will begin to roar as if it was an angry lion belting out, "Feed me! Feed me!" However, when God transitions us to fast, he specifies for us to not feed the flesh. When we think of the word *fast*, literally we think of cutting out food—the candy, chips, hot dogs, cake. We often misinterpret the Word. Fasting is not meant for you to lose weight, just for your personal pleasures or to prove to family and friends that you could do it. Fasting is not meant for you to fit in that dynamic wedding dress, prom dress, or summer outfit of your dreams. The purpose of a fast is to rid the body of the deadly toxics that it is carrying, such as sin. Sin is a deadly toxic, and if a person continues to satisfy their flesh being in sin, in the end the deadly toxic will begin to spread, and before they know it, after it has spread, it will produce death—spiritual death and/or physical death.

Another thing that the flesh produces is ignorance, but the spirit produces true wisdom, knowledge, and truth. Ignorance is a deadly disease such as cancer that eats up the body; ignorance clogs up the mind, but it can be broken through lots of fasting and prayer. It is very imperative for the believers to fast; what you can't do, God can. God is requiring that you fast so that the desires of the flesh can die. For some people, their desires might be glutting food or glutting objects such as cars, clothes, shoes, or money, but don't get me wrong; God wants for us to have things that we can enjoy such as cars, clothes, shoes, and money, but what he doesn't want for us to do is put these things ahead of him. I find it a huge problem when a person constantly tries to get more things into their homes but do not use the things they already have. We must realize that *whatever we feed will grow larger in our life.* If we continue to keep feeding the flesh, the flesh will grow into a monster. But now is the time for us to feed our spirit with the word of God!

Some people highly believe that fasting only requires for them to turn the plate down for a day—lay off on the Snickers bar—but feeding the flesh is far more than consuming food. Fasting can also mean to turn from things that will distract you from getting closer to God. This means that whatever is distracting you from getting closer to your heavenly Father, that is what you need to turn down.

You may be stuck in the middle of Satan's web looking for a way out, but I truly know that God will give you the full manuscript of how to break out and in victory. Fasting is very powerful. Fasting can destroy the chains of the enemy who devises a plan for you. For the enemy figures that if he can get your focus off God, then that will grant him the opportunity to have his way in your life. But when you set your attention on God, you are prompt to gain more wisdom, knowledge, and strength. The enemy, Satan, is after each and every one of you, and for this reason you must stay in your word. A person's lack of studying the Bible will allow them to believe every voice that comes their way; however, it is God's word that stops Satan and his cohorts in their tracks, not our words alone.

An important key that you must realize is this, "*The only way the enemy can get the best of you is when he finds there is no word inside of you to defeat him.*" If there is no word inside of you, your power source is worthless!

PUT GOD'S WORD INTO YOUR LIFE!

Flesh is one thing that God will not permit into his kingdom. In order to receive our place in heaven, we must be born of God's spirit, and we must make no provision for the flesh. Not only does the flesh have to die sometimes, but this is something that has to be killed on a daily basis. Temptations, lust, and every evil work of sin has all got to die! The flesh has to die of bad attitudes, bad habits, and old cycles that keep repeating itself; however, fasting, praying, and reading the word are good ways to stay connected to God and to break the repeated cycles of failure. Each one of us needs to live a life consecrated before God in fasting because this is a good way that we can draw closer to God and to stay connected to his spirit.

Are you tired of doing the same crazy things over and over again? Are you ready for the repeated cycles of failure to cease? Today you can live a life free from the cycles of the enemy! Today you can die from the flesh and receive life through the spirit! However, the word of God shows us the importance of the spirit and how imperative it is for us believers to walk in it. Also, God lets us know in his word that when we worship him, we must be willing to do it by his spirit for there is no other way that we can worship God but in spirit and in truth. Whenever the Holy Spirit directs us, he gives us the wisdom and knowledge we need in order to go in the right direction; but when we follow after the desires of the flesh, we will always make a huge mistake.

> And Jesus said unto them, It is not for you to know the times or seasons, which the father hath put in his own power. But ye shall receive power, after that the spirit is come upon you and ye shall be witnesses unto me both in Jerusalem, and in all Judaea, and in Samaria, and unto the utter most part of the earth.
>
> Acts 1:7–8 (KJV)

> Blessed is the man that walketh not in the
> counsel of the ungodly, nor standeth in the way
> of sinners, nor sitteth in the seat of the scornful.
>
> Psalm 1:1 (KJV)

> No man can serve two masters: For either he
> will hate the one, and love the other; or else
> he will hold to one, and despise the other. You
> cannot serve God and mammon.
>
> Matthew 6:24 (KJV)

> For to be carnally minded is death; but to be
> spiritually minded is life and peace. Because the
> carnal mind is enmity against God. for it is not
> subject to the law of God, nor indeed can be.
>
> Romans 8:6–7 (NKJV)

This is the time to get a new *mind-set* in your new
life! A born-again believer cannot mix their old ways
of thinking into their new life in Christ. With a new
life comes a new mind, and from having a new mind,
you have a new talk, and in you having a new talk, a
new walk comes out of that. We cannot meditate on
the miraculous things of the spirit if we are in the flesh,
nor can we meditate on things of the flesh (the carnal
mind) if we are in the spirit. The spirit and the flesh are
always in a battle against each other, and we as children
of God must use our spiritual eyes of discernment to
distinguish between the two.

I truly believe that many people can allow things to
flow smoothly into their life if they yield to the perfect

will of the Holy Spirit; however, those who are not in tune to the Holy Spirit the way they should be, the devil will always have them acting in the flesh. However, one way a person can find themselves defeating the flesh is by humbling completely to the Holy Spirit. The Holy Spirit is a keeper, and he will lead you into all truth. It is not God's will for his children to suffer being defeated by the devil; however, it is his perfect will that we prosper according to 3 John 1:2 KJV. Allow the Holy Spirit to come into your new life; for he wants to dine with you and know that *where the Spirit of the Lord is, there is liberty.* Also know that where the Spirit of the Lord is, there no sin can dwell.

> Beloved, I wish above all things that thou mayest prosper and be in health, even as thy soul prospereth.
>
> 3 John 1:2 (KJV)

The only way the devil can get the best of you is when he finds there is no Word inside of you to defeat him.

Living a prosperous life is a choice that everyone has to make, but the problem is that some choose to not live a prosperous life. In this life, there are only two ways a person can walk in, and they are the *spirit* or the *flesh.* And if we walk by the spirit, we will receive the wonderful gifts of the spirit—the fruits of the spirit—but if we walk by the flesh, we will receive the negative attributes of the flesh. What you put in is what you'll get out. If you sow to the flesh, you will receive things of the flesh, which include arrogance, pride, depression, oppression, and fear; but if you sow to the spirit, you will receive the wonderful things of the spirit, which include peace, joy, love, happiness, wealth, and perfect health. There is a fight that we must go through in our daily walk, and the only way to find ourselves walking in total victory is by denying one of our two components.

This is not the time for any more excuses because where you are now is the time to go all the way in God like never before! You have a decision to make; the choice is yours. So choose wisely who you will serve this day!

BATTLE IN THE MIND

Beloved, do not believe every spirit, but test the spirits to see whether they are of God; for many false prophets have gone out into the world. By this you know the spirit of God: every spirit which confesses that Jesus Christ has come in the flesh is of God, and every spirit that does not confess Jesus is not from God. This is the spirit of the antichrist, which you heard was coming, and now is in the world already. Little children, you are from God, and have overcome them; for he who is in you is greater than he who is in the world. They are from the world; therefore they speak from the world, and the world listens to them. We are from God. Whoever knows God listens to us; whoever does not know God does not listen to us. By this we know the Spirit of truth and the spirit of error.

1 John 4:1–6, ESV

W e are in crucial times of the Antichrist emerging. Many are traveling to and fro portraying to be of the truth, but what worries me the most is that many Christians are starting to believe them. The word highly speaks that in the end times, many will give heed to false teachings. There are false prophets in the world today preaching a happy message that will keep more money flowing into their church rather than correcting people of the wrongs that can send them straight to hell. For the enemy knows what people want to hear, and he will speak soothing words to try to persuade many to him. Now, individuals that have been saved for many years are questioning if the true Savior really exists. I can truly say that the word of God is being revealed.

If only the world can really see what Satan is trying to do to us! It's time that we know Jesus for real, not just talking the word, but showing the word through our actions. Religion alone won't save us, but having a personal relationship with Jesus will. There is a war going on, and it's starting with our mind for the mind is where God downloads the light of truth. The enemy is out to harness our thoughts because he knows that we are only one thought away to having victory. Our mind needs to be hidden so far in God that the enemy will have a very difficult time trying to find it.

In what state of condition is your mind in? Or in what condition have you allowed Satan to put your mind in? You need to know in this life that the condition of your mind will change. When you change, so does your mind. Not only do you change when your mind changes, but your identity changes too—and it is your identity that determines the type of character you really have. You have to be at a place in God where the enemy won't even bother coming in. Let your mind be so much on the word (the truth) that the enemy won't even try to send his lies your way.

> Keep thy foot when thou goest to the house of God, and be more ready to hear than give the sacrifice of fools: for they consider not that they do evil.
>
> Ecclesiastes 5:1 (KJV)

LET YOUR MIND BE HIDDEN SO FAR IN GOD THAT THE ENEMY WILL LITERALLY HAVE TO FIND IT!

When you are always thinking on the negative, you place God in a box, and that allows doubt to come in. and you will be surprised to know that a lot of them are Christians. Now can you believe that! It's as simple as this: we all know the scripture that says, "Now faith is the substance of things hoped for, the evidence of things not seen" (Hebrews 11:1, KJV). Well, let me tell you that if you can't see your breakthrough in advance and there isn't enough faith built up in your spirit to believe that it is coming, then that plainly means that you have a wondering mind, simple as that!

Remember, spiritual warfare has a major part to do with the mind. For the battlefield is not in the church, not in the streets, but in the mind. The mind is where the enemy makes his attack. But the good news is that you have the power to cast down every evil imagination that Satan shoots at you.

Let the mind of Christ rule in your mind so strong until the enemy can't bombard it with crazy thoughts ever again.

> For verily I say unto you, That whosoever shall say unto this mountain, Be thou removed, and be thou cast into the sea; and shall not doubt in his heart, but shall believe that those things which he saith shall come to pass; he shall have whatsoever he saith. Therefore I say unto you, What things soever ye desire, when ye pray, believe that ye receive them, and ye shall have them.
>
> Mark 11:23–24 (KJV)

In other words, Mark 11:23–24 is saying this: if we believe without wondering, we will get whatsoever our hearts desire. The problem with many in this generation today is that they want the blessings of the Lord, but they refuse to do whatever it requires in order to receive them. As being a part of the inheritance of God and being one of his child, you must realize that the same power and authority God has, it has been passed down to you; but don't nearly think that sitting at home watching television all day will get you where you need to be. This Christian walk requires many major commitments—some are turning away from food, less time talk on the phone, less time watching reality shows on television, and spending more quality time with the Lord. For spending time with the Lord will get each and every one of us where we need to be. But the reason as to why some don't receive the desires of their heart as soon is because of laziness, when all God asks is for everyone to rise up, start walking, and take our blessings by force.

The problem with some churches today is that an enormous amount of people in the church that are sitting on the church pews every Sunday do not want to move to get anything. Many of them expect God to come their way and throw blessings right in their hands, but it's not that easy! This is the time for you to stop sitting down comfortably on the church pew, resting from what God has called you to do and for you to get going! If you do not want to complete your work in ministry, Satan will be very pleased to take it.

> A new heart will I give you and a new spirit will I put within you, and I will take away the stony heart out of your flesh and give you a heart of flesh. And I will put my spirit within you and cause you to walk in my statutes, and you shall heed my ordinances and do them.]
>
> Ezekiel 36:26–27 (AMP)

> But ye shall receive power, after that the Holy Ghost is come upon you: and ye shall be witnesses unto me both in Jerusalem, and in all Judaea, and in Samaria, and unto the uttermost part of the earth.
>
> Acts 1:8 (KJV)

> Now the natural man receiveth not the things
> of the Spirit of God: for they are foolishness
> unto him; and he cannot know them, because
> they are spiritually judged.
>
> 1 Corinthians 2:14 (KJV)

OBEY THE SPIRIT WITHOUT DOUBTING!

On many occasions in my life, I have gone through situations where I had to literally choose to do something. I took some time to meditate on it in my mind until I came up with the answer; then, after making my decision, in the end I realized that I had made the wrong choice by not getting God's approval in the first place. However, going by my own free will instead of God's will for my life led me in the wrong direction. Many have been just like me doing their own thing. But why do we constantly refuse to hear the voice of the Lord? In every situation that we have, we ought to ask God for direction. He knows the right road we should take.

> And Elijah came unto all the people, and said,
> How long halt ye between two opinions? if the
> LORD be God, follow him: but if Baal, then
> follow him. And the people answered him not
> a word.
>
> 1 Kings 18:21 (KJV)

> O thou of little faith, wherefore didst thou
> doubt?
>
> Matthew 14:31 (KJV)

Faith is produced directly by the spirit. Faith and salvation work hand in hand. However, the enemy doesn't want our mind and our spirit both to agree; he knows that if we can change our mind from thinking negative thoughts to positive thoughts, then he can no longer take control over our minds. One of the enemy's greatest tools is to get our attention off God; he knows once he has our mind, he can get us any way he pleases. This is why we must guard our mind with the word of God. We must also realize the battle is not with our family, nor with our friends, nor with our haters, but in our mind! For where the mind goes, the man follows.

In the book of Matthew, Peter noticed Jesus was walking on the water. Peter was amazed when he noticed the Messiah standing along the water, and Peter's prime intentions were to get to Jesus. And so Peter stepped out of the boat along the water, and he began to walk—not focusing on anything around him but on Jesus. Peter's focus was not on the rest of the people in the boat but on the one who was before him.

Meanwhile, as Peter was getting closer to Jesus, fear began to sit in because of the waves that were rushing and being intense; and before Peter knew it, he began to sink. Satan figured that if he could get Peter's mind from focusing on Jesus, then he would have him completely. This is exactly what Satan wants to do to you and me; he wants to get our focus off Jesus, the Author and the Finisher of our faith, and get us to focus on the waves of the water—trials, temptations, agony, pain—and how deep the water is so that we will sink. Satan knows that in Jesus our future is great, and he will try to throw all types of obstacles in the way to stop us from walking out on the water. This is what he says, "If I can just get through their mind, I know I will have them!" If Satan can get to our mind, he can hinder our prayers, our praise, our worship, and our time in the word. He wants to keep us locked in boat position so that we won't step into the water of success. But I am here to say that if you are reading this book, now is the time for you to walk out on your water in faith! Don't allow the enemy to speak to your mind saying you are going to sink. You are not going to sink.

Satan may have lied to you and told you that your ministry, business, marriage, and relationships are all going to sink, but God told me to tell you that everything you do will succeed! Though there might be times where it seems like you are sinking a little in the water, the good news is that Jesus is there to lift you back up. Satan is after your mind, but Jesus came to give you peace.

I am here to stand in total agreement with you reading this book, that as you read it even now, I apply the blood of Jesus to cover your life. I command the Word of God to penetrate deep into your mind, your body, and your soul. No longer will you be defeated by the devil, but you will defeat him!

> Meanwhile, the boat was far out to sea when the wind came up against them and they were battered by the waves. At about four o'clock in the morning, Jesus came toward them walking on the water. They were scared out of their wits. "A ghost!" they said, crying out in terror. But

Jesus was quick to comfort them. "Courage, it's me. Don't be afraid." Peter, suddenly bold, said, "Master, if it's really you, call me to come to you on the water." He said, "Come ahead." Jumping out of the boat, Peter walked on the water to Jesus. But when he looked down at the waves churning beneath his feet, he lost his nerve and started to sink. He cried, "Master, save me!" Jesus didn't hesitate. He reached down and grabbed his hand. Then he said, "Faint-heart, what got into you?" The two of them climbed into the boat, and the wind died down. The disciples in the boat, having watched the whole thing, worshiped Jesus, saying, "This is it! You are God's Son for sure!"

Matthew 14:24–32

After this there was a feast of the Jews; and Jesus went up to Jerusalem. Now there is at Jerusalem by the sheep market a pool, which is called in the Hebrew tongue Bethesda, having five porches. In these lay a great multitude of impotent folk, of blind, halt, withered, waiting for the moving of the water. For an angel went down at a certain season into the pool, and troubled the water: whosoever then first after the troubling of the water stepped in was made whole of whatsoever disease he had. And a certain man was there, which had an infirmity thirty and eight years. When Jesus saw him lie, and knew that he had been now a long time in that case, he saith unto him, Wilt thou be made whole? The impotent man answered him, Sir,

> I have no man, when the water is troubled, to
> put me into the pool: but while I am coming,
> another steppeth down before me. Jesus saith
> unto him, Rise, take up thy bed, and walk. And
> immediately the man was made whole, and
> took up his bed, and walked: and on the same
> day was the sabbath.
>
> John 5:1–9 (KJV)

Thirty-eight years is a long time for anybody to have to wait to be healed. Aren't you glad that Jesus took away your every last infirmities when he died for you on the cross? Jesus died a painful death on the cross so that you and I could be healed. Some may say, "Well, I know that Jesus died for me to be healed, but why am I still suffering with my illness?" Well, let me ask you a question: have you given your sickness completely to Jesus? Completely giving your sickness to Jesus will require for you to give him your mind, your body, and your soul. There cannot be any part left in you that can be used as a deadly tool for Satan's pleasure.

> My people are destroyed for lack of knowledge:
> because thou hast rejected knowledge, I will
> also reject thee, that thou shalt be no priest to
> me: seeing thou hast forgotten the law of thy
> God, I will also forget thy children.
>
> Hosea 3:6 (KJV)

Having wisdom and knowledge is not based on how well a person speaks. Having wisdom and knowledge is not in how intelligent a person may look; on the other hand, knowledge is not for anyone to show they know everything. However, God made us with two ears to do more hearing and one mouth to do less talking. True wisdom requires true wisdom because it teaches you what to say and what not to say. The ones standing alone from the crowd always receive the more, and why is that? Because while others are spreading their business, the ones who are standing alone are listening and taking notes on what and what not to do. You must be highly aware of people who are quiet because they make the ones gagging at the mouth seem really foolish. "The way of a fool is right in his own eyes: but he that hearkeneth unto counsel is wise. A fool's wrath is presently known: but a prudent man covereth shame" (Proverbs 12:15–16, KJV).

Jesus was like the quiet ones: while people said harsh words about him, he remained calm. But what people did not know was that he was going to give the same negative talkers salvation at the end. The same ones who spoke cruel words about Jesus were the same ones that needed him to wash away their every sin.

Now can you imagine for someone to hate the very ground you walk on, but in the end, they will need you to be there to lend them a helping hand? A lot of us will not be there for our enemies; nevertheless, show them love when they don't love us. But Jesus's love was so great toward his enemies that he was willing to die for them so that they could be set free.

The enemy stirs up mess by the words a person says out of their own mouth. Many times he will seduce a person by using their own weapons against them. If a person doesn't know something, it's best for them to be quiet. Put the word of God into your life.

> My son, attend to my words; incline thine ear
> unto my sayings. Let them not depart from
> thine eyes; keep them in the midst of thine
> heart. For they are life unto those that find
> them, and health to all their flesh.
>
> Proverbs 4:20–22

Meditating the word of God in your mind will actually affect your physical body.

Meditation brings healing to your spirit as well as your physical body.

Focus on the scripture Isaiah 53:5 that says by Jesus's stripes you are healed, healing will take place in your body. Whatever you focus the most on will eventually focus on you. In Mark 4:24, if it's not of God, then tune it out! You have to learn to guard your mind, your ears, your mouth, and your eyes against the enemy. Don't allow negativity to bring you down any farther than where you are. And remember, "For they that are after the flesh do mind the things of the flesh; but they that are after the Spirit the things of the Spirit" (Romans 8:5, KJV).

If you walk in the spirit, you will not think on flesh-defeating thoughts. There is absolutely no way you can have a life of abundance with a negative mind! In Matthew 12:33 of the Bible, it tells us to either make the tree good and his fruit good, or else make the tree corrupt and his fruit corrupt: for the tree is known by his fruit. Since a tree is known by its fruit, you and I are known by the way we think. You can tell the way a person's life will end up by what they are thinking. Our thoughts describe exactly what will come into our life.

Godly thoughts bring supernatural blessings into our life; thoughts of the flesh, on the other hand, produce corruptible things into our life. The word of God has to be placed in our hearts daily in order to receive a deposit from it. We cannot keep getting withdrawals from something if no deposit is being made. You cannot go to the bank and constantly ask for withdrawals from money that you have never put in; you will always have insufficient funds. This is why there are lots of people who are trying to succeed off another person's gift, not only in the church, but throughout the world. Why does this happen? This happens because the one who is trying to pimp off another individual's gift hasn't put anything in to receive what the anointed one has. For we will find in the book of Acts that Simon beforetime used sorcery and bewitched the people of Samaria. However, after Simon saw the works of the Holy Ghost working through the apostle's hands, he offered them money.

> But there was a certain man, called Simon, which beforetime in the same city used sorcery, and bewitched the people of Samaria, giving out that himself was some great one: To whom they all gave heed, from the least to the greatest, saying, This man is the greater power of God. And to him they had regard, because that of a long time he had bewitched them with sorceries. But when they believed Philip preaching the things concerning the kingdom of God, and the name of Jesus Christ, they were baptized, both men and women. Then Simon himself believed also: and when he was baptized,

he continued with Philip and wondered, beholding the miracles and signs which were done. Now when the apostles which were at Jerusalem heard that Samaria had received the word of God, they sent unto them Peter and John: Who when they were come down, prayed for them, that they might receive the Holy Ghost: (For as yet he was fallen upon none of them: only they were baptized in the name of the Lord Jesus.) Then laid they their hands on them, and they received the Holy Ghost. And when Simon saw that through laying on of the apostles' hands the Holy Ghost was given, he offered them money. Saying, Give me also this power, that on whomsoever I lay hands, he may receive the Holy Ghost. But Peter said unto him, Thy money perish with thee, because thou hast thought that the gift of God may be purchased with money. Thou hast neither part nor lot in this matter: for thy heart is not right in the sight of God. Repent therefore of this thy wickedness, and pray God, if perhaps the thought of thine heart may be forgiven thee. For I perceive that thou art in the gall of bitterness, and in the bond of iniquity. Then answered Simon, and said, Pray ye to the Lord for me, that none of these things which ye have spoken come upon me.

Acts 8:9–24 (KJV)

The Holy Ghost was operating fully in the Bible as we see in the book of Acts and is still working today. Jesus declares in his word that after the Holy Ghost shall come upon you, you shall receive power. This means that without the Holy Ghost, we are powerless. This scripture tells us that after the Holy Ghost comes upon us, we shall receive power, not before. We cannot fight the enemy in our own strength.

Jesus lets us know in the word that it is best if he goes away because if he doesn't go away, the comforter will not come. The comforter is his Spirit, the Holy Spirit. Jesus died for you and went back to the Father just so you could receive the Holy Spirit and the free gift of salvation into your life. If you have not received your free gift yet, you can receive it today. But I have a question: when you receive your gift, what will you do with it? How can someone expect to ever know who Jesus really is if they never study the Bible for themselves? The Word—the Bible—is God's heart and mind to us written down on paper. The more you study the Bible, the more knowledge you will gain on what God likes and what he does not like; furthermore, as you read the word, you will understand Gods' perfect will for your life (Jeremiah 1:4–5, 29:11, and Isaiah 43:1).

> This book of the law shall not depart out of thy mouth; but thou shalt meditate therein day and night, that thou mayest observe to do according to all that is written therein: for then thou shalt make thy way prosperous, and then thou shalt have good success.
>
> Joshua 1:8 (KJV)

THE WORD MEANS SUCCESS; NO WORD MEANS NO SUCCESS!

The word of the Lord produces success, but if you do not take out the time to learn the word, you will find your life going in the wrong direction. The word of the Lord is our daily map that will help us get to our destination. What is our destination? Our destination is heaven. Heaven is a place where we are trying to get to, but how can we find our way there to that wonderful place if we do not take out the time to study our map and instructions, the Holy Bible, for ourselves?

The devil, on the other hand, cannot stand the word; he knows the word, but he cannot handle it. The devil also knows that if he can steal the word of God out of our mouth, he will be able to steal our total power source. Also, what it is that every believer must realize is that prayer cannot be effective without the Word of God. However, we must learn to pray the word of God instead of praying our problems, our frustrations, and our worries. When we pray the Word—God's promise—despite of our many life's experiences, the prayers that we pray in faith sabotage the enemy's domain.

When Satan thought that he was going to create a gigantic mess of the world (to try to pollute it with his seed), God used his word to bring the world back into proper order. The seed that Satan thought that he was going to spread and plant in the earth, later God sent his Son, Jesus to the earth that he might destroy the works of the devil. One thing about God is that he is a positive God; he speaks words that are of great benefits to our everyday life. Another thing that I like about

God is that he has given his children the same power to speak positive words into our atmosphere. As children of God, we can make a major change in our life for the better by changing the way we think and by changing the words that come out of our mouth. I found to be true that the way we think determine the words we say, and the words we say do determine the life we live. If you find yourself living a terrible life, today you can live a prosperous life full with abundance of joy, peace, and wealth by changing your words and thoughts! Don't just accept everything the devil brings your way. You have the power to reverse every negative word that the devil has ever told you. It's time that you separate the good seed from the bad. You can use this scripture as a total guide to take into consideration when you think about saying negative words out of your mouth:

> Death and life are in the power of the tongue,
> and they who indulge in it shall eat the fruit of
> it whether its life or whether it is death.

Proverbs 18:21 (KJV)

Consider this moment a brand-new start in life. Start walking in the fullest of Christ by being submissive to his Spirit. Begin to speak what you want from the Lord; decree and declare that it is already yours, and watch it manifest in the earth realm. So throw away the doubt, and from this day forward, walk by God's Spirit!

WE ARE UNDER ATTACK

For the weapons of our warfare are not physical [weapons of flesh and blood, but they are mighty before God for the overthrow and destruction of strongholds, [Inasmuch as we] refute arguments and theories and reasonings and every proud and lofty thing that sets itself up against the [true] knowledge of God; and we lead every thought and purpose away captive into the obedience of Christ (the Messiah, the Anointed One), Being in readiness to punish every [insubordinate for his] disobedience, when your own submission and obedience [as a church] are fully secured and complete.

2 Corinthians 10:4–6, AMP

S atan devises a horrible plan for every one of us, and his closet is full of schemes that he tries to use to destroy every marriage, relationship, and church. Does this make you exempt from his weapons? No. We are not exempt from Satan's weapons at all. As a matter of fact, Satan's main objective is to destroy every believer as well as every nonbeliever. He wants to weaken strong individuals especially within the Christian church so that we won't come together in unity to do the work of the Lord more effectively. What he does is try to weaken each member of the body of Christ one by one, and when they begin to do the work of the Lord, they do not have enough strength to complete it. Satan wants to tire our bodies out with work and with other unproductive things that are in our lives that when we come to church throughout the week to worship, what we offer God is our leftovers. We should not make our only time to worship God the days we attend church, but every day should be a time of worship and praise. The demonic realm is highly waiting for the moment to capture individuals, so we must praise and worship God until all of Satan's powers are completely destroyed! It's time that we destroy the plots of the enemy through our praise! As Satan is busy, we have to also be busy by doing the work of the Lord.

Satan does not like you. He doesn't care about you being wealthy, nor does he care about you being poor; all he is concerned about is you worshiping him. There is a strongman that is lurking through our churches, communities, businesses, and homes, and if we do not recognize him and place him where he belongs, he will contaminate everything that is around him. It's time for us to become strong soldiers in this army and not weak individuals who are always defeated by the enemy and life circumstance. When we speak about the strongman—the evil one—it is very imperative that we place on the whole armor of God that will guard us from his every attack.

> Finally my brethren, be strong in the Lord and in the power of His might. Put on the whole armor of God, that you may be able to stand against the wiles of the devil. For we do not wrestle against flesh and blood, but against principalities, against powers, against the rulers of darkness of this time, against spiritual hosts of wickedness in heavenly places. Therefore take up the whole armor of God, that you may be able to withstand against the wiles of the devil and in the evil day, and having done all, to stand.
>
> Ephesians 6:10–13 (NKJV)

Do you know of the plans that Satan has for your life? Because he is after your life and he needs to be bound. If you know the strongman you will know of his schemes, tricks, and his many lies. Unfortunately Satan's plan for you is nothing good; his plan is to kill, to steal, and to destroy. He constantly plots of schemes for your demise. However, when you determine the strongman that is in your life, it is highly important that you also address his weapons. Many people who have dealt with spiritual warfare in the past were binding up the enemy, but they were not binding up the many cohorts of demons that he brought along with him for the ride.

Whenever you are engaging in spiritual warfare and before you bind the devil, you must first recognize what other demons you are going to be with that spirit and then you must bind them both up and then shoot for the attack. When the enemy shows up, he doesn't just come by himself. In many instances on a busy street if you see one duck crossing the street, you better believe there are going to be a whole line of other ducks behind that one duck. Just like the line of ducks, the devil has his lineup of demons to follow when he comes in. One of the worst things that a person can do when dealing in spiritual warfare is to bind up a demon without binding up the subordinate spirits that are also involved. When a person is dealing in deliverance, the person must bind and loose every evil work out of the demon possessed individual's life, and not only that, but that person must also bind and loose those demons that lay dormant inside of the person. I have been in some deliverance services in the past where a person, who was possessed by a demon, would go to the altar for deliverance, and as they were being delivered, the pastor who was doing the deliverance service would take them hours before the demon was cast out of the possessed individual. Meanwhile, as the pastor was praying over the individual, the church would be also interceding for the individual. After hours of working and sweating, the demon would finally come out of that person. Weeks later, the person who was being delivered from the demonic influence would come back to church, and once again the devil will act out. Many times the demon would run rapidly throughout the service as if they never were fully delivered.

I began to wonder why some people that were being delivered from a spirit would come back to church weeks later and the demon would act out once again. Some of the reasons why this would happen is because they were comfortable in doing the wrong that they were doing. If a person does not want to be free, the demons will linger. The way the possessed get free is by first admitting that there is a problem and secondly relying on Jesus as their ultimate source to deliver them.

Some pastors are trying to cast out demons and the reason why they are not coming out immediately is because they are trying to call out one demon by name and cast it out when there are other demons that need to be called out and cast out as well.

It is very imperative for those dealing in spiritual warfare to rely totally on the Holy Spirit to reveal to them the reason of some ones struggles. How will you be able to know what a person is dealing with if you are not spiritually aware to what is going on? However, those people who are looking for deliverance or who is engaging in the deliverance must recognize what it is that brought a particular demon into the person's life, once the person recognizes the different demons that are in their life they can then cast them out. They must do whatever it takes to get rid of a demonic spirit and much of it requires lots of fasting and prayer.

It's time that you bind up every work of the devil
and leave none of his works unchained. Let me ask
you a question "What strong man have you bound up
lately?" Did you just bind up the devil himself, or did
you bind up all of his buddies as well?

> And I will give unto thee the keys of the
> kingdom of heaven: and whatsoever thou shall
> bind on earth shall be bound in heaven: and
> whatsoever thou shalt loose on earth shall be
> loosed in heaven.

Matthew 16:19 (KJV)

Not only is binding important in spiritual
warfare, but loosing is also important. Jesus shows
the importance of binding and loosing as shown in
Matthew 16:19 as well as in Matthew 18:18. We have
to use our binding and loosing methods that God has
given us to defeat the enemy from out of our lives. We
must also know that we have gates to our spirit, soul,
and body. The Holy Spirit seals our spirit, but we can
still be oppressed in the spirit. Sometimes in life we will
feel a little down-and-out, but the Holy Spirit comes
to give us peace and complete joy. We need to learn to
shut all open gates against the enemy; however, walking
in righteousness is a way that every believer can keep
their gates closed, but "when we are not walking in
righteousness, our gates will be opened and our bars
will be devoured by fire" (Nahum 3:13). It tells us that
walking in righteousness will keep us in the presence of
the Lord. However, when we are not walking upright
the way the Lord wants us to, we step outside of our

boundaries of protection into an area where Satan can do what he wants to with us; and when we step outside of our boundaries of protection, before you know it, fear, disbelief, depression, and anxiety will all come in to take a seat into our lives.

> Whoso breaketh an hedge, a serpent shall bite him.
>
> Ecclesiastes 10:8 (KJV)

It is imperative that we keep our gates closed to the enemy and our mind opened to God. We cannot give the enemy the privilege to come into our minds in anyway. Well, you may ask this, "How do I keep my gates closed?" can keep your gates closed by staying in God's word—being obedient to his word, fasting, and daily meditating in prayer. Prayer is a key principle in the lives of the believers in order to live a successful life. Prayer must become our way of life not just only when we need God to work something out for us, but every day we are mandated to pray. For the Bible declares that men are to always pray. The enemy is after God's children and prayer is one way that we can defeat him. There is a fight going on! This fight is not with the flesh or with blood, but this is a spiritual fight against principalities and rulers of darkness of this world. The Apostle Paul tells us to pray always. Ephesians 6:18, KJV, says, "Praying always with all prayer and supplication in the Spirit, and watching thereunto with all perseverance and supplication for all saints." This fight is against things that are unseen to the human eye.

Have you ever heard the saying, *I was born to fight*?
Many think that these are just traditional words that
people love to use, but these are words that I actually
find to be true. However, Satan will continue to fight us
as long as we are in the earth, he will not stop until he
does all that he envisions to do. But we believers are not
ignorant of Satan's devises so this means that we must
fight for our family, for our loved ones, for our friends,
and for our church. We must stand strong in battle and
stop allowing the enemy to defeat us.

> The mighty one, God, the Lord, speaks and
> summons the earth. Out of Zion, the perfection
> of beauty, God shines forth. Our God comes,
> He does not keep silence, [neither should we]
> before Him is a devouring fire, round about
> Him a mighty tempest. Psalm 50:1–3 (KJV)

We have to pray the victory before the fight. I am
not referring to a physical fight but a spiritual fight:
praying the victory before the fight refers to us, and
praying the promises of God instead of us praying our
worries, frustrations, or failures. When you know what
God has promised you and you are highly holding on
to that promise, you do not have to worry because the
answer is already in your hand; all you are doing is just
waiting for the manifestation. Also, when you know
who Jesus is in your life and who you are in him, you
do not have to fight the battle because he has already
defeated Satan at the cross just for you; for the battle
belongs to the Lord, but he is requiring something

from you and that is, for you to pray, praise, and become obedient to his command. And when you have done all these three things, you can sit back and relax knowing that the Lord is in complete control and anything that is under his control will never be out of control.

Having the Lord in my life has given me the courage to relax, not worrying about a thing, knowing that he has me covered 100 percent for my trust is not in man but in God as stated in Psalm 51. I also have the courage in knowing that the blood of Jesus will cover me from the enemy's attacks.

PRAYER CHANGES THINGS!

Prayer brings on many changes, but prayer cannot take full affect without true love. We have much power in God that all we have to do is speak a word, and things will start to change before our eyes. However, Satan opposes love because he knows that this is another powerful tool that we have in order to defeat him. In order for our prayers to flow unhindered in the realm of the spirit, we cannot have any alt or animosity against our brothers and sisters in the Lord. Love is a godly principle that God has given us to follow; he even shows us in his word how to love others.

"What are you carrying in your mouth?" Do you know that words carry power? Often, seemingly it appears that instead of us using our mouth for the good, we use it for the bad on many occasions. Many speak hateful words against their brothers and sisters, not realizing that there is a load of power behind them.

> But ye shall receive power after the Holy Ghost
> has come upon you.
>
> Acts 1:8 (KJV)

> The power of the Holy Ghost is flowing active
> today as it was in the Bible days. Jesus declares
> in the book of John, "For I have not spoken on
> my own authority; but the Father Who sent me
> gave me a command, what I should say and what
> I should speak. And I know that His command
> is everlasting life. Therefore, whatever I speak;
> just as the Father has told me, so I speak.
>
> John 12:49–50 (KJV)

God gives us power when we actually need it; he
gives us power to speak words that can change the
atmosphere around us for the better. However, some
people use their power for the wrong reasons, and
instead of them speaking loving words of power, they
speak negative words against their brothers and sisters
in the Lord. But the power that God has given us was
not given for us to speak hurtful words that can break
down someone's life, but to speak positive words that
can build someone's life up. Reading the Word of God
and quoting Scripture is a good way for us to exercise
our vocabulary the right way.

The world was framed by the spoken word of God.
Nothing would be in existence if it wasn't for God's
word. When God said "Let there be light!" light didn't
take a couple of minutes to arrive on the scene, but
immediately light was brought forth. Because of God
(the Word) speaking light into a void world, it caused

everything that seemed void to come to life. God's word is life. However, we need the word of God in our daily life. We cannot live without the word; for God is the word, and in him we live, we breathe and have our being.

Also, we must realize that each and every one of us cannot make it without God's Spirit; for the Holy Spirit gives us strength, and once the Holy Spirit begin flowing active in our lives we have to keep getting more of him. Just like a cell phone battery cannot go all day without being charged, this is exactly how we are, spiritually. We need a recharging of the Holy Spirit for our everyday lives. No one can continue to operate in ministry without getting a recharge, a spiritual boost to keep going, from the Holy Spirit. It is through the Holy Spirit that we receive power.

Readers, you must also know that you cannot go into spiritual warfare without receiving a total connection from the Holy Spirit. That is why it is important that you stay connected to the Holy Spirit so that you won't lose your spiritual power. We do not and cannot fight the enemy in our own strength; every time we do, we will be defeated. We can stay connected to the Holy Spirit as we pray. The Bible lets us know that when we pray in the Holy Ghost—our heavenly language—we confuse the enemy. Praying in the Holy Ghost is a great tool that we all can use to allow God to hear our prayers. Furthermore, the more we pray in the Holy Ghost, the more power we will receive. It's time for us to receive a recharge!

Are you at a place where it seems like you can't pray, fast, or worship like you used to? There is a short circuit in there somewhere. If you don't have the joy like you used to have, then that means that it's time for you to recharge. Don't go on any further living a Christian life with your battery on low. Now is the time for you to reconnect with God like never before. You have been running off of the same spiritual battery for quite some time. Now is the time that you reconnect to your Power Source, God!

The enemy is out to steal what you have been given, but the Holy Spirit will destroy all of the enemy's works. You must always remember it is the anointing that destroys the yoke. Isaiah 10:27, KJV: "And it shall come to pass in that day, *that* his burden shall be taken away from off thy shoulder, and his yoke from off thy neck, and the yoke shall be destroyed because of the anointing."

MAKING A TOTAL CONNECTION

1. Charge yourself up in the Holy Ghost by staying in daily devotional prayer. Talk to your heavenly Father and tell Him what's on your mind. (Jude 1:20 KJV)
2. Spend time in the Word daily to hear what the Lord has to say (that means throwing away your opinion). Meditate on the Word on a daily basis and stay in-tuned to His Spirit to receive further instruction.
3. Being faithful in ministry by doing what God has transitioned you to do.

4. Spend time in praise, worship, dancing, clapping, singing, silence. For more insight, read the book of Psalm.

The only way the enemy can get the best of you is when he finds there is no Word inside of you to defeat him.

In this life there is a daily struggle that we have to face. We were born in a world of sin, but every fight is not intended for us to fight. There is one fight that God instructs for everyone to fight, and that is the fight that Paul spoke about: "Fight the good fight of faith, lay hold on eternal life, whereunto thou art also called, and hast professed a good profession before many witnesses" (1 Timothy 6:12). One thing you must know we cannot make it without fighting this fight of faith that the Bible speaks on is a fight of believing that what God said is going to happen and will happen! This fight is what separates the victors from the victims, the losers from the winners, and the believers from the doubters. This fight is what will determine if you end up on the top or if you end up on the bottom. Along with this fight on a daily basis we are fighting for this flesh of ours to die. We are urged to fast and pray until our flesh is not defeating us. Many times we blame everything on the devil when it is our own flesh that needs to come in subjection to the spirit of God. As we spend time in our weapon (the Word), the flesh will not be able to get the best of us in any way. Also in this daily life that we live, we must stay in prayer for the answers that the Lord has promised us will come; as a matter of fact, we must wage war in prayer so that the answers can come to us manifested and with great results.

There was a man in the Bible by the name of Jacob who wrestled with an angel for a while and was not going to stop the fight until he received an answer from the Lord. Jacob was persistent in the line of his divine duty to fight, and he prevailed because he didn't lose hope.

> But during the night he got up and took his two wives, his two maidservants, and his eleven children and crossed the ford of the Jabbok. He got them safely across the brook along with all his possessions. But Jacob stayed behind by himself, and a man wrestled with him until daybreak. When the man saw that he couldn't get the best of Jacob as they wrestled, he deliberately threw Jacob's hip out of joint. The man said, "Let me go; it's daybreak." Jacob said, "I'm not letting you go 'til you bless me." The man said, "What's your name?" He answered, "Jacob." The man said, "But no longer. Your name is no longer Jacob. From now on it's Israel (God-Wrestler); you've wrestled with God and you've come through." Jacob asked, "And what's your name?" The man said, "Why do you want to know my name?" And then, right then and there, he blessed him.
>
> Genesis 32:22–29

You need to wrestle with God until he comes through for you! Don't waiver in your faith, but stand firm on the promises that he has made to you and know that he is faithful to do exactly what he said. Don't be afraid to pull on God in prayer. Allow God to recognize you in prayer so that he can think about you and bless you even when you aren't asking for anything.

In prayer this is where you build up your power source to defeat the enemy. So I urge you to stay down on your face in prayer to God! I also urge you to stay persistent in the word so that you can maintain your deliverance.

We must realize that the word is what's going to keep us in the midst of everything that is going on around us. It is the word that will sustain us in the midst of trials and situations. In this life we face many battles, but the battles are won not through our physical fights but with the word. As Satan has a line of demonic forces that are lined up to attack, we have the word as our weapon and God standing to back us up. Whenever we enforce our authority with the word, heaven stands in agreement. Gods' word is the only thing that will stand. If you are ever in attack by the enemy, don't be afraid to stand your ground and use your weapons! Don't be afraid to *put your foot down*! Don't be afraid to use the word! God wants us to trust solely on him; he wants us to depend on him with our marriage, with our finances, in our business, and with our health. God wants us to know that despite of the many circumstances that we face, he will come through.

Matthew 10:16–24 (KJV) shows us exactly why we should fight; it says,

> Behold, I send you forth as sheep in the midst
> of wolves: be ye therefore wise as serpents, and

harmless as doves. But beware of men: for they will deliver you up to the councils, and they will scourge you in their synagogues; And ye shall be brought before governors and kings for my sake, for a testimony against them and the Gentiles. But when they deliver you up, take no thought how or what ye shall speak; for it shall be given you in that same hour what ye shall speak. For it is not ye that speak, but the Spirit of your Father which speaketh in you. And the brother shall deliver up the brother to death, and the father the child: and the children shall rise up against their parents, and cause them to be put to death. And ye shall be hated of all men for my name's sake: but when they persecute you in this city, flee ye into another: for verily I say unto you, Ye shall not have gone over the cities of Israel, till the Son of man become. The disciple is not above his master, nor the servant above his lord.

In the day of prosperity be joyful but in the day of adversity consider: God also hath set the one over against the other, to the end that man should find nothing after him.

Ecclesiastes 7:14 (KJV)

During our times of war, we have a comforter who will be there and who we can call on that will give us peace despite of the blocks that are in the path. For Jesus declares in the book of Matthew that we are supposed to fight. At times we will have to go through persecutions, trials, and temptations in this Christian walk, but with Jesus on our side, everything will work out for our good. But how can a person depend on someone if they never need their help? The fights that we face arc not all intended for us to fight; we are to depend on God in every fight that we face.

> Think not that I am come to send peace on earth: I came not to send peace, but a sword. For I am come to set a man at variance against his father, and the daughter against her mother, and the daughter in law against her mother in law. And a man's foes shall be they of his own household. He that loveth father or mother more than me is not worthy of me: and he that loveth son or daughter more than me is not worthy of me. And he that taketh not his cross, and followed after me, is not worthy of me. He that findeth his life shall lose it: and he that loseth his life for my sake shall find it.
>
> Matthew 10:34–39 (KJV)

> The Lord is near to all who call upon Him in truth. He will fulfill the desire of those who fear Him; He also will hear their cry and save them. The Lord preserves all who love Him, but all the wicked He will destroy.
>
> Psalm 145:18–20 (KJV)

> The Lord is far from the wicked, but He hears the prayer of the righteous.
>
> Proverbs 15:29 (KJV)

Many families have been set apart by the enemy. Studied research shows that there are far more women in church every week than there are men. Churches around society today are packed out with a huge amount of women; the events consist of women, from women conferences, women luncheons, women brunches, to women cruises. But where are the men in the midst of the events? They are at home watching their favorite basketball, football, baseball, or boxing team play on television. Then when the wife leaves from her outing with the other women in the church, she arrives home too tired and too worn out to spend time with her husband. However, the enemy's primary goal is to separate families; he does not want unity to abound. As long as the women in the church are having their events separate from their spouse, that is all okay with the enemy; but it's time that married couples come together in unity. It's time that the husband and the wife come together as one and pray for their family, pray for their marriage, and pray for their salvation with God. I guarantee that if we pray and put our loved ones in the hands of the Lord, there will be a total change. Satan does not want for families to come together on one mind and on one accord in the Spirit that is why he tries his best to separate many families apart. One thing Satan hates the most is for individuals to walk together in unity because where unity abounds, strength also abounds. When believers pray together something miraculous happens. Jesus says in the Scriptures:

> Again I say unto you, That if two of you shall
> agree on earth as touching anything that they

shall ask, it shall be done for them of my Father which is in heaven. For where two or three are gathered together in *my* name, there am I in the midst of them.

Matthew 18:19–20 (kjv)

The Number One Target of the Enemy

One of the enemy's targets that you need to know is that he wants to keep the children of God bound, and the way he binds us is by his many lies. Satan's target is to demolish the church as a whole. He is after the leaders in the body of Christ and out to attack to rest of the body because if he can get to the leader, which is the head, the rest of the body will be out of place because the body cannot function with a screwed up head. What Satan does is try to stir up envy and strife in the church allowing the members and the leaders to fight one another so that they will focus more on fighting each other, instead of spending most of their time praying.

Satan doesn't want unity to flow unhindered in the church. He knows that if the church comes together in unity, they can tear his kingdom completely down. We can use the men in the book of Joshua as a prime example. These men came on one mind and on one accord when they marched around the city praising the Lord. Because of that, Jericho's wall came tumbling down during the seventh time they had marched around the city. I don't think people understand the importance of unity. Unity breaks down the kingdom of darkness. When we are walking in one mind and in accord with the Spirit, we are blocking the path of the enemy.

Another weapon that the enemy uses is this weapon of hatred amongst the body of Christ. This is a huge monster, and it must be completely destroyed! However, instead of believers coming together in unity everyone is trying to do their own thing. God's word shows us the importance of unity and where each one of us is to be fitted into the body.

> Now there are diversities of gifts, but the same Spirit.
>
> Romans 12:4 (KJV)

> For as the body is one and has many members, but all the members of that one body, being many, are one body, so also in Christ. For by one spirit we were all baptized into one body. For in fact the body is not one member but many.
>
> 1 Corinthians 12:12–28 (KJV)

We are one body in Christ and functioning with one purpose, and that is to please God. Since there is only one body in ministry, we must take care of the body and disengage any demonic attacks against it. As the natural body has many parts, so does the church body. If I were to simplify it, it would be like this: it starts with the pastor forming the head, and the church forming the rest of the body; however, if the head is jacked up and not fully functioning the way that it should, the whole body will be messed up as well. Why is it that many have lost the fear of God? It's time for the fear of God to return back to the church. The church should not be functioning out of place, because in order for Satan to be exposed and bound up, we must function in an orderly manner. It should not be that the members of the church are telling the pastor what to do and what they are going to do. This is all a form of witchcraft. The church needs to return to true holiness as the Bible speaks about. The church has to come back into proper order according to the word of God. For God is not the author of confusion—Satan is!

Satan (Lucifer) was created for perfection. He was the best at many things; however, he brought division into the kingdom of heaven, and eventually later on God kicked him out along with the one-third host of angels that went with him. From the very beginning of time, Satan has been plotting up division against the saints. It is his primary tool to separate the people of God from their place of authority. He wants what he once had, and that is authority. Satan is after our soul. He wants to be our god, and if we are not highly careful, he will try to trick us into believing that we can make it a whole lot better if we served him. But the devil is a liar! We will not bow down to the enemy! We will not bow down to his lies or his seducing plots! For Jesus is Lord of our lives!

Lucifer was in God's holy place and had everything that he could possibly need. Everything that he had God has given him, but he wanted more authority—he wanted to set himself above the throne of God.

When people talk about Lucifer, the way they would envision him is being mean, rude, ugly, dumb (without knowledge), and arrogant; however, Lucifer was far more than that! Lucifer was full of wisdom and perfect in beauty. Lucifer had everything around him and inside of him; he was made with the most fantastic singing voice that you can ever imagine. There were pipes in him with all types of instruments, also the most precious stones that you can ever imagine were his covering: the sardius, topaz, and the diamond, the beryl, the onyx, the jasper, the sapphire, the emerald, and the carbuncle, and gold (Ezekiel 28:13 KJV).

Can you imagine these beautiful stones aligning someone's garments! Now if Lucifer had everything there was and was anointed by God, what more could he need, and what more could he want? Lucifer was one of God's archangels, so this means that all angels are not great benevolent creatures. (At that time, we will be higher than the angels, and we will even judge them.) The Word of the Lord says, "Do ye not know that the saints shall judge the world? and if the world shall be judged by you, are ye unworthy to judge the smallest matters? Know ye not that we shall judge angels? How much more things that pertain to this life?" (1 Corinthians 6:2–3, KJV).

Many think that all angels are great benevolent creatures, but we must realize that some of God's angels rebelled against him, and for that reason, they too will one day be judged along with us.

If all angels were created holy as God is holy, then what really happened?" The Bible indicates that at some point, Lucifer, one of Gods' angels, rebelled against him and was eternally terminated from heaven:

> Moreover the word of the Lord came unto me, saying Son of Man, take up a lamentation upon the king of Ty-rus, and say unto him, Thus saith the Lord God; Thou sealest up the sum, full of wisdom, and perfect in beauty. Thou hast been in Eden the garden of God; every precious stone was thy covering, the sardius, topaz, and the diamond, the beryl, the onyx, and the jasper, the sapphire, the emerald, and the carbuncle, and gold: the workmanship of thy tabrets and of thy pipes was prepared in thee in the day that thou wast created. Thou art the anointed cherub that covereth; and I have set thee so: thou wast upon the holy mountain of God; thou hast walked up and down in the midst of the stones of fire. Thou wast perfect in thy ways from the day that thou wast created, till iniquity was found in thee. By the multitude of thy merchandise they have filled the midst of thee with violence, and thou hast sinned: therefore I will cast thee as profane out of the mountain of God: and I will destroy thee, o covering cherub, from the midst of the stones of fire. Thine heart was lifted up because of thy beauty, thou hast corrupted thy wisdom by reason of thy brightness: I will cast thee to the ground, I will lay thee before kings, that they may behold thee. Thou hast defiled thy sanctuaries by the multitude of thine iniquities, by the iniquity of thy traffick; therefore will I bring forth a fire from the midst of thee, it shall devour thee, and I will bring thee to ashes upon

the earth in the sight of all them that behold
thee. All they that know thee among the people
shall be astonished at thee: thou shalt be a
terror, and never shalt thou be any more.

Ezekiel 28: 11–19 (KJV)

BEWARE OF WOLVES IN SHEEP'S CLOTHING!

What caused the one-third host of angels to be cast
down to the earth along with Satan? This is a question
that a lot of you may be very anxious to know. The
reason why the one-third of angels was cast out of
heaven and will one day be judged is because they
followed Lucifer. Lucifer led one-third host of heaven
to stop worshipping God, to observing Lucifer's beauty.
But what it is that you must realize is that, whoever
your leader is you will follow them, and if the one who
is leading is headed in the wrong direction you as a
follower will be going in the wrong direction as well.
However, if you follow Satan for too long he will show
you the way to hell. But you have to make sure that you
are not following Satan, or an agent of him, but that
you are being led by the Holy Spirit.

The one-third of angels that were cast down to earth
has followed the wrong leader and because of that, they
are no longer angels of God but Satan's demons. Every
demon that has ever bothered you in your life once had
a place in heaven, and now that they have been kicked
out of Heaven, they now have a place prepared for them
in the lake of hell's fire.

The word "Devil" comes from the Greek *diabolos*, which means accuser. Satan is a Hebrew word meaning "adversary". In Christianity, the devil is the source of evil and the chief foe of God and man. The ancient Hebrews believed in demons or evil spirits.

During the middle Ages, people viewed the devil as a tempter who was always near, always enticing them to sin. They thought it was possible for a person to sell his soul to the devil in exchange for worldly gain or supernatural power. In art the devil was often shown as a grotesque animal or a man with horns, hoofs, and a tail.

When we look at a wolf to our terminology, it will be that it is black or gray, with very sharp teeth, with very sharp nails; however, when we define a sheep, we will consider it being sweet, gentle, and easy to be trusted. When we come into contact with a sheep, we must be really sure that it is a sheep and not a wolf. However, there are many wolves appearing in the world, and they are appearing in sheep's clothing, but we must highly recognize the sheep from the big black wolf.

Have you ever been in a relationship where the person thought that they were in complete control? The person began to control who you talked to on the phone and who you associated yourself with; they even took it a step further and controlled the clothing attire that you had on so that the cloths you had on wouldn't be too spectacular to another individual's eye that it would catch their attention.

What about this one? Have you ever been in a ministry where the pastor thought that he or she were in total control to the point that they would place fear in you and instead of you obeying God, you would obey the pastor because you were afraid of them? This is exactly where Lucifer went wrong. Lucifer wanted complete control over everyone, but God put him in his place and let him know who was boss. We have to beware of leaders who are not preaching the kingdom of God to lead others to Christ but are preaching and twisting the Scripture to lead others to them so that they can control them.

Satan wants to turn our church into a place like Burger King, where we can have it our way; but you need to realize that if it's not God's way, then there is no way! We cannot have it our way for we are not in control. Many churches around society today have been turned into a circus with bunch of wild animals, a slavery camp full of slaves, and a personal bank for pastors to get their members money for their own personal use. But it shouldn't be!

Church has been turned into a competition to see who knows who, who has what, and who does what. Church should not be a place for Satan to dwell but should be a place that is highly sanctified for God.

Now is the time that we clean up the church! This is the time that we clean up the gossiping, the hatred, jealousy, strife, manipulation, and intimidation! Can we just throw all differences aside? Can we forget about who knows who, who has what, and get to know Jesus for real! All throughout the Bible it speaks on Satan's downfall—pride was a major area in his defeat. One day Satan will be cast into hell's fire for all the lies he has ever told, for all the people that he tried to destroy. But now Satan is using what's left of his time to try to deceive many for he knows that his time is almost up.

One thing I found about serving God is that he is in complete control; for our times are all in the Lord's hands. God is the potter and we are the clay. The thing about a potter is that they can do whatever they want to do with their clay, and they can shape it into whatever shape they want it to be in. Since God is the Head Potter and we are his clay, he can shape us into whatever image he will like us to be.

The word *serving* means assisting, rendering, ministering, giving aid, or service. We each have to serve somebody, but the problem is that no one wants to serve anymore—everyone wants to be a leader. However, before we can become a leader, we have to serve somewhere. We have to become servants of God—having a humble spirit to do his will and in us serving him, he will bless us for our loyalty and commitment. We must serve God in our worship, in our praise, and in our giving tithes and offering. Those who serve willingly will always have a humble spirit. True servants are never arrogant, prideful, or boastful about themselves. True servants never have an *I* or *Me* attitude. However, there is a demonic spirit that has been trying to creep its way through the church—this is the spirit of pride and arrogance. The spirit of pride and arrogance is trying to creep its way right into the church pews, but we must pray and combat this evil spirit from out of our land and from out of our church. For the Scriptures let us know that we should always stay humble. God tells us this, that if we humble ourselves before him, he will exalt us in due time. God did not intend for man to exalt themselves above him nor did he intend for us to boast about things that we have done (just like Lucifer did), but that we allow all of our boasting to be all on him.

Lucifer was a boaster of himself. Lucifer boasted on all the things that he had, and no one could tell him anything different. He knew that he was the bomb! Don't get me wrong, God does want for us to encourage ourselves, and sometimes we will be in a situation where no one will speak good things about us, and we will have to speak good things about ourselves with words like: I am more than a conqueror! I am an overcomer! I am somebody! I am rich and all of my needs are met! However, there is a gigantic difference when we tell someone, "I can do this a whole lot better than you! I am very good at what I do! I am somebody, and you are not! These are words that sound similar to that of Lucifer. But what really made Lucifer mess up was when he tried to over-rank his authority and set himself above the throne of God. What some people do not know is that when they exceed the authority that they have been given, they are headed for a gigantic fall and for the pastors who are scattering their flock, God says, "Woe unto them!"

When issues are not confronted they leave a gap open for the enemy to take full advantage, then sooner or later the gigantic monster of pride and arrogance is formed, and not only is the victim being abused; but the abuser has also been abused, and the only way the abuser can find some ease is by abusing another individual.

If you are going through abuse or any other problem, realize you have a problem and confront it! For God loves both the abuser and the victim of abuse; for you must realize that there is hope beyond abuse!

God has a way out of any abusive relationship that you might be in just stay in prayer and the Lord will reveal with you the way to get out. No one wants to live under abuse for years and decide to get out once you are on your dying bed. I have encountered many people who have gone through or are going through abuse on a daily basis, and these individuals whom I have spoken to would say "I don't know how to get out!" One of the ways to get out is to just open up the door and leave! You can determine if you are going to stay in an area of abuse or you can determine if you do something about it! Make up in your mind today to say No to abuse!

EXPOSING THE UNSEEN ENEMY

Is there an explanation to why there is so much violence? Is there an explanation to why there is so much sickness? Is there an explanation to why there is so much confusion? Yes there is an explanation, but you need to know exactly who it is that is causing a lot of these things to happen. There is an unseen enemy that is unseen to the natural eyes, but you can see him through your spiritual eyes of discernment. This unseen enemy is out to kill, to steal, and to destroy. This is the same one that presented himself to Adam and Eve in the garden of Eden. This is the same one that presented himself to Jesus as he was in the wilderness. This is the same one who filled Judas [the betrayer] heart to betray Jesus. We are talking about Satan, the prince of the power of the air. His objective is to pollute the world with his seed. However, the Holy Spirit is here to show each and every one of us Satan's weapons and He is here to block them when they come and to stop Satan's seeds from sprouting. Satan does not have legal access to operate here in the earth so we have the authority to place him back where he belongs as the word says in Matthew 18:18 and in Matthew 16:19.

> How art thou fallen from heaven, O Lucifer, son of the morning! How art thou cut down to the ground, which didst weaken the nations! For thou hast said in thine heart, I will ascend into heaven, I will exalt my throne above the stars of God: I will sit also upon the mount of the congregation, in the sides of the north: I will ascend above the heights of the clouds; I will be like the most High. Yet thou shalt be brought down to hell, to the sides of the pit.
>
> Isaiah 14:12–15 (KJV)

> And there was war in heaven: Michael and his angels fought against the dragon; and the dragon fought and his angels, and prevailed not; neither was there place found any more in heaven. And the great dragon was cast out, that old serpent, called the Devil, and Satan, which deceiveth the whole world: he was cast out into the earth, and his angels were cast out with him.
>
> Revelation 12:7–9 (KJV)

Since Satan does not have legal access to operate in the earth realm, all his works here are illegal. Satan is doing illegal activities in the earth and we have to legislate our authority over him in Christ. Just as God is spirit, the Holy Spirit, and can be invited in, Satan is also spirit, an evil spirit, and can be invited in. However, the way a person allows Satan to come in is by invitation or through given permission. Satan cannot harm God's children unless he first allows. Every day Satan, the accuser of the brethren, is standing before God to judge the believers; he says this: "God, do you remember what they did before they found you!" Satan stands before God accusing us not on something new that we have done, but on old sins that God himself has forgotten about. But thanks be unto God for sending his Son, Jesus—being made manifested in the flesh— that he might destroy the works of the devil.

We must also realize that every attack we face is not always orchestrated by the devil. The Lord has his reasons for every trial that comes our way. Sometimes the Lord will take us through a test to see how we will respond to being in it. Look at the story of Job in the Bible. Job was an upright man who had a pure heart, but Job had to encounter a lot of storms in his life. The storms that Job encountered taught him the greatness of God and that what he was in was only temporary because he knew of the power in the God that he served. In the end because Job didn't charge God foolishly, God restored back to him all that he lost and a whole lot more.

You need to realize that the minute you became saved you have begun a test, and God is the score keeper. He keeps the score to your walk and obedience to him. However when Satan the tempter comes, God is requiring that we past every test of temptation that he brings. Whenever we past a test in this life, that entitles for us to receive a total blessing from the Lord; however, every time the enemy comes our way God is testing us to see if we will remain at peace during the storm; for everything we do is being scored in heaven. Every time we press our way to church even in times when we don't feel like going, God is writing down a score. Every time we are faithful to ministry and serving our pastors without murmuring and complaining, God is writing down a score. But the question that I will like to ask you is, *do you measure up to receive God's perfect score?*

> For I was an hungered, and ye gave me meat: I was thirsty, and ye gave me drink: I was a stranger, and ye took me in: Naked, and ye clothed me: I was sick, and ye visited me: I was in prison, and ye came unto me. Then shall the righteous answer him, saying, Lord, when saw we thee and hungered, and fed thee? or thirsty, and gave thee drink? When saw we thee a stranger, and took thee in? or naked, and clothed thee? Or when saw we thee sick, or in prison, and came unto thee? And the King shall answer and say unto them, Verily I say unto you, in as much as ye have done it unto one of the least of these my brethren, ye have done it unto me.
>
> Matthew 25:35–40 (KJV)

> For God is not unjust to forget your work and
> labor of love which ye have shewed toward His
> name, in that ye have ministered to the saints,
> and do minister. And we desire that every one
> of you do show the same diligence to the full
> assurance of hope unto the end: That ye be not
> slothful, but followers of them who through
> faith and patience inherit the promises.
>
> Hebrews 6:10–12 (KJV)

REMEMBERING THE YOUNGER DAYS

You have to visualize your walk in God as being levels of the spirit. As in primary school, a child goes from kindergarten to the twelfth grade; spiritually, this is quite the same. The higher you go in God should show how mature you would become. Paul says it best, "When I was young I spoke as a child." Many look at this text and automatically think that it means growing from a child into an adult; however, this was not what Paul was talking about. What Paul was saying was, "The more knowledge that I have obtained, I began to live according to that knowledge."

When a person first gets saved, there will be a lot of things that they will not know about salvation. However, the thing about a newborn is that at a certain time in their developing process they will begin to ask questions like "Why is this?" or "Why is that?" On the other hand, a newborn in Christ starts their Christian walk by asking questions like: "How do I pray?" "How do I communicate with God?" "What does God like, and what does He dislike?"

> Are you a Christian who is stuck in Park Position, or are you a Christian who is ready for drive?

When you come to a level of maturation in God some of these questions, you will already know. There is no specific age limit for a person to act like a child. Some individuals are past sixty and still acting like a child. However, the acting I am speaking of is from a spiritual perspective; when no growth is being established in our life we will become complacent—thus acting like a child. Unfortunately, some people are still in preschool, and they're not little anymore.

When we become a Christian, we should not think that Christianity just stops there; but in our Christian walk, we are to go from glory to glory. Never should there be a time for us to believe that we have fully arrived to the area that we need to be in God. There is a place that God is trying to get His people but He cannot get them there why they are trying to make adjustments in the wilderness; because what happens in the wilderness stays in the wilderness!

WHAT HAPPENS IN THE WILDERNESS, STAYS IN THE WILDERNESS!

This is not the time for you to bring the wilderness into the promise land. All wilderness dreams, all wilderness objectives, and all wilderness passions have all withered away; now is the time for you to walk into the new!

Some blessings that God gives us will require for us to be in the right location in order to receive them. And with each new location that God takes us, there will be a new blessing awaiting us there. But when a person is stuck in one particular place for a very long period of time, they will eventually become bound to that location. Now is the time that you get out of your comfort zone and possess the land! Now is the time that you to get up from the place that you are bound and move!

There are many reading this book that may have been stuck in the same position for many, many years, but now is the time for you to get up and move! It's time that you get out of Egypt and move into your promised land!

Ask yourself this question: am I a Christian stuck in park position, or am I a Christian that is ready for drive? We have to make up in our minds to get ready for drive position and refuse to let the enemy keep us locked in the same position forever. There is a great plan that God has in store for each and every one of us, but we cannot allow the enemy to snatch it away when we get it.

In the thirteenth chapter of the book of Matthew, Jesus came on the scene to teach the people about the parable of the sower. It was in this parable that Jesus was trying to get the people to understand that with this word of mine that you have received, you have to guard it in your hearts, because there is an evil one

who is coming to try to steal it. Jesus knew that the
people weren't fully grasping what it was that he was
saying. Had it been that they fully grasped it that they
could recognize when the thief was coming to steal the
seed that was sown. Jesus tells them in the text in the
fourteenth verse of that chapter, "Hearing you will hear
and shall not understand, And seeing you will see and
not perceive; For the hearts of this people have grown
dull" (Matthew 13:1–23, KJV).

It was not too long after many of the people received
the word that it was stolen from them by the evil one.
You cannot let the enemy steal all that has been planted
on the inside of you. On the inside of you lies great
success and the devil knows it, and that is why he is
trying to depress and oppress the people of God, so
that they can abort their divine purpose in being here.
There are many people who are in the grave today who
had greatness on the inside of them, and now they
aren't able to use any of it! There are people who could
have been the next billionaire with a great invention,
but they are not here today. What it is that you must
realize is that the minute God promises you something,
the enemy can't stop it from happening, but what he
can do, is set obstacles in the way. Many of the people
in the text in Matthew, had the Word of God, received
it with joy, but the devil came and snatched it causing
them to lose everything that they had.

The children of Israel could not fully recognize their
place of victory already before they have physically seen
it. There were many remarkable people that could have

gone to the Promise land that was allotted to them, but however, many of them got lost during the transition.

Will you allow the enemy to cause you to abort the destiny that is within? Will you allow the enemy to influence or control your every move? Will the enemy be the cause of you not reaching your full potential in God? I don't know about you, but I refuse to be like the Israelites who waited forever to get their blessings because of disobedience. The Israelite's flesh—fear, disbelief, and complaining—kept them in park position, when they should have switched gears a long time ago. We have to get out of our comfort zone—our place of comfort—and start moving in the many wonderful and miraculous things that God has in store for us!

> Behold, I have set the land before you: *go in and possess the land* which the Lord sware unto your fathers, Abraham, Isaac, and Jacob, to give unto them and to their seed after them.
>
> Deuteronomy 1:8 (KJV)

WHAT GOD PROMISED THEM, HE PROMISED US THE SAME!

> And Caleb stilled the people before Moses, and said, Let us go up at once, and possess it; for we are well able to overcome it. But the men that went up with him said, We be not able to go up against the people; for they are stronger than we.
>
> Numbers 13:30–31 (KJV)

Before I go any further, let me tell you this, that whenever God gives us the instructions to do something, He always gives us the right resources that we need that can help us in doing it. God tells us things to do for a specific reason. However, God will not allow anyone to do something that He knows they can never do. When the Lord instructed the Israelites to take dominion over the promise land that He was giving them, He gave them everything they could possibly need in order to get there; and with this came the ability for them to take full possession; however, the men that went up with Caleb to view the land that God promised to give them began to doubt saying, "We are not able to go up against the people, for they are much stronger than we!" But what each and every-one of you must realize is that *your thought life can produce good seed or it can produce bad seed.* You are only one thought away from receiving the life you desire. Those who say words like *I can't* will produce bad seeds into their life, but those who say words like *I can* will produce good seeds into their life; the ones that planted good seed out of their mouth, before they know it the seed will grow into a spectacular tree producing many blessings.

> And all the congregation lifted up their voice, and cried; and the people wept that night. And all the children of Israel murmured against Moses and against Aaron: and the whole congregation said unto them, Would God that we had died in the land of Egypt or would God we had died in this wilderness! And wherefore hath the Lord brought us unto this land, to fall

by the sword, that are wives and our children should be a prey? were it not better for us to return into Egypt? And they said one to another, Let us make a captain, and let us return into Egypt. Then Moses and Aaron fell on their faces before all the assembly of the congregation of the children of Israel. And Joshua the son of Nun, and Caleb the son of Jephunneh, which were of them that searched the land, rent their cloths: And they spake unto all the company of the children of Israel, saying, The land, which we passed through to search it, is an exceeding good land. If the Lord delights in us, then he will bring us into this land, and give it us; a land which floweth with milk and honey.

Numbers 14:2–9

Doubt and fear allows many to wander in the wilderness. When God speaks we should do exactly what he is requiring for us to do. When the spirit of the Lord speaks, run with it. however, the reason why some find themselves going backward instead of going forward is because of disobedience; and the reason why they cannot comprehend God's voice from the rest is because they have ignored the first spoken words of God. By the time God spoke and passed by, they have allowed other voices to flow active in their mind and later, the voice that has been planted, have invited other voices to join and has created a whole symphony of voices.

How do I know when God is speaking? Have you ever heard a voice calling your name that you tried to distinguish that calling? Have you ever heard your name called by someone that you knew really well, but it just so happened that you were amazed to find that they weren't the one who was calling?

Many times I have heard my name being called by someone, and the voice sounded exactly like my mother's voice. However, when I responded, "Mom, did you call me?" She replied, "Boy, no, I didn't call you!"

"Mom, but it just sounded like your voice!" I replied.

I just knew it had to be my mother's voice. From the day I was born, I knew my mother's voice. But sometimes, the Lord comes to us sounding like someone who we are familiar with hearing. My mother would tell me that whenever I heard my name being called in a way that I have never heard before, that it was the Lord calling to tell me something, just as he did to Samuel in 1 Samuel 3:1–21.

Samuel did not know the voice of the Lord, and so when the Lord called him, he went to Eli because Eli's voice was the only voice that he was familiar with. But after Samuel kept running back to him, Eli perceived that it was the Lord who was calling him.

How do I know God's voice from Satan's? John 18 gives us this answer. "My sheep know my voice, and a stranger they will not follow." Also, someone prophecies to you God will either tell you first or he will confirm to you what he is saying through his word or through another believer; however, when a prophecy has been given, and it is totally different from what you said that God told you in the first place, one of the voices can only be God—that is if his word is in it.

One thing that I like about God is that he never changes, and what he says in his word will remain the same for all eternity. In him are his words, "Yea" and "Amen." God expresses how powerful his word is when he says that "So shall my word be that goeth forth out of my mouth: it shall not return unto me void, but it shall accomplish that which I please, and it shall prosper in the thing whereto I sent it" (Isaiah 55:11, KJV). However, refusing to hear the voice of the Lord will allow many doors of sin to open, and once the doors of sin have completely been opened, they will allow for the spirit of bondage and many familiar spirits to come in. Familiar spirits can be with a person for so long that they will begin to put on a form of the person, portraying who they really are. Familiar spirits are best known for mocking something or someone; however, I will talk more on familiar spirits later throughout the book.

There are great doors of opportunity that God allows us as believers to walk through, and we have to be fully loaded with the word. There are going to be some demons that will be sent out on specific assignments to try to make us change our mind: from thinking on the promises of what God said to thinking on negative things and issues that we are going through in life. We have come way too far to go back to Egypt! The promise land is waiting for us, but we have to find the way there by staying in the Word; for the Word is our map and compass to take us to our promise land. As a car cannot be driven all day without gas, we cannot get to the promise land driving on empty fuel. Our inner-man must be fully loaded with gas the *Word*, fuel *the Holy Ghost*, and a proper battery *prayer* and *fasting*. We must stay totally charged up and fueled up in the Holy Ghost, and we must stay in the word of God to receive further instructions.

Unlike the Israelites, the Lord told them he was giving them a land to take by force; but because of disobedience, they had to wait in Egyptian bondage for nearly four-hundred years. After that, the Lord eventually led them to their promise land, however, most died along the way. In this walk, we need to have spontaneous faith, and not only that, but we have to also align ourselves with faith-filled people. For it takes true faith to follow faith! Do not follow anyone who does not have the faith of God; for you must always remember that Satan is a god of doubt, and if someone is around you who are always in doubt, be aware of them because they might just be special agents of the enemy.

Will you bow down to the spirit of doubt? Will you allow doubt to hinder you from walking into your season of blessings? This is the time that you put doubt down and walk by God's Spirit! The battle is in the mind but you have the powerful in the Holy Ghost to take full control of your mind, your thoughts, and your words. This is the time that you stop allowing Satan to lead you in the wrong direction, and allow the Holy Spirit to lead you in the right direction. This is the day that you break free from Egyptian bondage and walk freely into your promise land! For you are now free to do what God has called you to do!

Satan's Already Defeated

Over such the second death has no power, but
they shall be priest of God and of Christ, and
they shall reign with him a thousands years.
And when the thousand years are ended satan
will be loosed from his prison and will come
out to deceive the nations which are at the four
corners of the earth, that is, Gog and Magog,
to gather them for battle; their number is like
the sand of the sea. And they marched up over
the broad earth and surrounded the camp of the
saints and the beloved city; but fire came down
from heaven and consumed them, and the devil
who had deceived them was thrown into the
lake of fire and sulphur where the beast and the
false forever and ever.

Revelation 20:6–10, KJV

Byron Walker

The Lord tells us in the book of Jeremiah that he
knew about us even before we knew ourselves.
God tells Jeremiah that everything about him he
already knew. So since God knew about us from the
very beginning, guest who else knows about us? Satan
of course! Satan knows a lot more about some of us
then what we know about ourselves. He knows that
God has something great for each and every one of us,
and this is one reason why he fights us the way he does.
Satan knows that God has a great plan for our lives,
a great plan for our future, and his duty is to allow us
to get frustrated with church, frustrated with people,
and allow us to give up on God. Satan will use every
obstacle he can to try to block us from walking into the
blessings of the Lord.

Readers you must realize that Satan has no beginning;
the only thing that he has is an end; nevertheless, if
Satan tried to get right or tried to repent he couldn't
because God has no mercy over him, but as for you, you
have another chance at life. Aren't you extremely grateful
that God's mercy covers your life when sin counted you
out a long time ago? Somehow God, because of who he
is, because of his mercy, and because of his Son Jesus
shedding his blood, you have been given a brand new
start. When sin counted you out, God's mercy stepped
in and said "No! I have the final say in their lives!" For
the Lords mercy endures forever! However, God gives
every believer a fair chance to get where they need to be
in him; but as for Satan, he has no chance. Satan missed
a great opportunity of a life time when he tried to go
above God in the first place. Satan wanted to be in total

control because of the things that God gave him; but with the things that Satan had, he became prideful and arrogant in them.

Those who are reading this book, I am here to tell you that no matter where you have been, and no matter what you have done, God says that you can start all over again! It's now time that you put every weight, every sin, and every frustration aside and be born again in Jesus Christ! No matter what shape you are in, today can be the beginning of a new life just for you!

> Then I saw an angel coming down from heaven, holding in his hand the key of the bottomless pit and a great chain. And he seized the dragon, that *ancient* serpent, which is the Devil, and bound him for a thousand years, and threw him into the pit, and shut it and sealed it over him, that he should deceive the nations no more. Till the thousand years were ended. After that he must be loosed for a little while.
>
> Revelation 20:1–3

I have italicized the word *ancient* this word has been around for a very long time and has been used to refer to something that is very old in age. Also in this passage, it says that "Satan was bound for a thousand years." Therefore from reading this, Satan has neither authority nor freedom; however, the only authority that Satan has is the authority that we give him. Those individuals who are possessed with demons were not just selected as the enemy's choice, but they have given him an invitation to come into their life thus causing him to possess them.

Ever since Lucifer (Satan) has been kicked from heaven he's been trying to kill, steal, and destroy God's children seeking to get revenge. Since Satan cannot mess with God, he tries to get his children instead for a replacement. But thanks be unto God for sending his Son, Jesus, that when Satan does come in, you and I can employ the *blood of Jesus* to stand in his way.

HOW DO I KEEP SATAN OFF MY TRACKS?

1. Submit to God Resist the devil and he will flee from you (James 4:7, KJV).
2. Walk in the spirit, and you shall not fulfill the lust of the flesh (Galatians 5:16, KJV).
3. Be strong in the Lord and in the power of His might. Put on the whole armor of God that you may be able to stand against the wiles of the devil (Ephesians 6:10–12, KJV).

Many are aware that Satan's end is quit near. In the Bible it doesn't note when the actual day will be, but we know that the days are far approaching by the many evil activities that are going on in the world today. When you observe the news, you will find that people are being killed, robed, and sexually abused, and not only that, but there are so many negative reports being aired daily throughout the media and throughout the airways. The atmosphere is full of evil spirits, but God has given his children the power to bind and loose those evil spirits and change the atmosphere around them for the better. God has given his children total authority to declare liberty throughout the earth and to loose those that are bound. There is a real demon that has been sent out to destroy our churches, our families and our homes; and he will not stop without a fight. We have to proclaim our dominion in Jesus Christ by taking a stand against the enemy. We must be the ones that will take a stand for what is right because the Devil doesn't play fair, and neither should we. Satan will do all he can do to take a wide load of people to hell with him. Satan is after our soul because he does not want to suffer alone. Satan does not want to have to experience hell all by himself.

Do you know that Satan doesn't want to suffer alone? The reason why Satan is after you the way that he is—is because he lost something great, and he now has to suffer for it. When Lucifer was kicked out from heaven, the reason why he took some angels along with him was because he wanted them to share in the same punishment that he is going to get. However, there are many questions that people are anxious to know about hell and one of them is this, "Was hell made for God's children?" Understand this hell was never made for God's children. Hell was made for the devil and the fallen angels. While Jesus was on the earth his message was to preach the kingdom of heaven and for people to receive life through him so that they would never have to experience death and hell. After the time of Jesus death, he went to hell for us all, and the purpose of him going there was to snatch the keys away from Satan. Locked up in hell we were, but thanks be-unto God for sending his Son, Jesus in the likeness of flesh—but without sin—to snatch us out of the flames of hell. The love of Jesus is so real toward us that he does not want any of us to live in hell. The enemy is out to seduce many into thinking that hell is a wonderful place to be, but if a person thinks that they are experiencing hell right about now, they don't quite have a clue to the way hell really feels! Satan is bound, and he wants for everyone else to be bound with him.

The definition for Satan refers him as being the ruler of the air, not the earth. This means that the only way Satan can live is through flesh. Satan has no legal access to be here on earth, so for this reason we must send him back where he belongs—and that is under our feet. The only way Satan can possess an individual is by an invitation only. How do people invite Satan and his demons in? When people are sinning they widely give Satan legal access to come into their lives. If you do not want Satan to come into your life, don't partake in sin, because sin is a total invite for Satan and his demons. When a person invites Satan in, he always loves to bring his buddies along with him—those cohorts of demons. We must realize that demons are real! Demons are not just a figment of our imagination or something from a comic book strip, but they are very real indeed! However, when a demon is cast out of an individual, the person that is praying must also cast out the evil spirits that are associated with that particular demon as I have mentioned earlier. Some demons can follow a person from birth all the way into adulthood if they are not cast out. But can people that grew up in the church all of their life have demons? Yes they can. When you do not have on the whole armor of God, you are entitled to allow demons to use your body as a playground. Where there is no armor and no word inside of you, your spiritual temple is empty, and sooner or later, the enemy is going to see that no one is living there and he is going to move in.

Each believer should make sure that they give the Holy Spirit access to live inside of them. Also, each believer should make sure that they are feeding their temple with the bread of heaven, the word of God. The Word of God is what severs the head of the serpent, the enemy. You must realize that, the only way Satan can get the best of you is when he finds there is no word inside of your temple. And because the devil is always lurking for a body to use, we must learn to pray fervently and strategically. There is a war going on and we are in the center of it. Satan wants to keep God's children in total ignorance; and when you are ignorant of Satan's device that is when he can get the best of you. But God comes to give us wisdom by his spirit. The Holy Spirit will load us with the proper tools we need in order to defeat Satan in battle. We must also learn to pray more effectively—praying prayers that will demolish the kingdom of darkness. This is why the Scriptures say in Matthew 18:18 (KJV), "Whatsoever ye shall bind on earth shall be bound in heaven: and whatsoever ye shall loose on earth shall be loosed in heaven." Satan has no authority to be in the earth realm. Since Satan is bound he has no rights to be in your life, your church, your home, nor in your work place. The Bible doesn't give the time frame that Lucifer was kicked out of heaven, but if he presented himself in the Garden of Eden, to Eve, in the disguise of a deadly serpent, imagine how he will come to you and me!

> And God said, Let us make man in our image, after our likeness: and let them have dominion over the fish of the sea, and over the fowl of the air, and over the cattle, and over all the earth, and over every creeping thing that creepeth upon the earth. And God blessed them, and God said unto them, Be fruitful, and multiply, and replenish the earth, and subdue it.
>
> Genesis 1:26–28 (KJV)

The word *replenish* means to refill, restock, reload, replace, renew, and restore. God called forth man to replenish the earth; he called man to speak life to every dead situation that is in their life. God has given you authority to replenish everything that may seem to look dead in your life. You may be experiencing a dead situation right about now that seems as if what you put your mind to do is about to wither away, but the power is in your mouth to speak life over it. You don't have to live in a world of fear and torment any more. You don't have to be depressed about a plan that seems like it won't succeed; for the power is in your mouth to speak like!

As stated in the book of Genesis, after Satan's extermination from heaven, he produced a seed on the earth, and because of his seed, God destroyed the whole earth except for Noah. Because Noah was an upright man who feared God and was obedient to his command, God was gracious to save him along with his entire family.

> When men began to multiply on the face of the ground, and daughters were born to them, the Sons of God saw that the daughters of men were fair; and they took to wife such of them as they chose. Then the Lord said, "My spirit shall not abide in man forever, for he is flesh, but his days shall be a hundred and twenty years." The *Nephilim* [Giants] were on the earth in those days, and also afterward, when the Sons of God came into the daughters of men, and they bore children to them. These were the mighty men that were of old, the men of renown. The Lord saw that the evil of men was great in the earth. And then the Lord was sorry that He had made man on the earth, and it grieved Him to His heart. So the Lord said, "I will blot out man whom I have created from the face of the ground, man and beast and creeping things and birds of the air, for I am sorry that I have made them." But Noah found favor in the eyes of the Lord.
>
> Genesis 6:1–8

Back in the Bible days, there were giants in the land, and these giants came about through the seed of the fallen angels. I have underlined the words *giants* and *Sons of God*. If you were to really study the book of

Genesis, you will find that one-third of the angles that followed Satan came down to earth and put on the form of flesh. Many of the angels slept with the daughters of men and produced an off spring of giants, five of which are the following: *Anakims, Emims, Rephaim, Avims,* and *Zamzummins.* These races of giants can be found throughout the Bible.

As stated in the Bible, David had a fight with a giant by the name of Goliath. David slew Goliath not in his own strength, nor in his own ability, but he relied solely on the Holy Spirit. David knew that he was not capable of defeating Goliath himself. Just as David relied on the Holy Spirit, we have to rely on him as well to help us defeat every Goliath that is in our life. The only true way for a person to fight strategically in spiritual warfare is by totally relying on the Holy Spirit. The Holy Spirit is a total guide for those who are dealing in spiritual warfare. When a soldier is getting prepared to fight, he must have on the proper attire to fight successfully; however, when a soldier does not have on the proper attire and does not have the proper weapons with him, he is prompt to get hurt. Therefore, when we do not rely on the word and the Holy Spirit for our guide, we will constantly be defeated in battle.

> Then Jesus sent the multitude away, and went into the house: and his disciples came unto him, saying, Declare unto us the parable of the tares of the field. He answered and said unto them, He that soweth the good seed is the Son of man;

The field is the world; the good seed are the children of the kingdom; but the tares are the children of the wicked one; The enemy that sowed them is the devil; the harvest is the end of the world; and the reapers are the angels. As therefore the tares are gathered and burned in the fire; so shall it be in the end of this world.

Matthew 13:36–40 (KJV)

And I saw a new heaven and a new earth: for the first heaven and the first earth were passed away; and there was no more sea. And I John saw the holy city, new Jerusalem, coming down from God out of heaven, prepared as a bride adorned for her husband. And I heard a great voice out of heaven saying, Behold, the tabernacle of God is with men, and he will dwell with them, and they shall be his people, and God himself shall be with them, and be their God.

Revelation 21:1–3 (KJV)

Your Goliath has to come down, he cannot stand! You must know the bigger your Goliath is, the harder he will fall. Your Goliath may be sickness, but know that it has to come down! Your Goliath may be blocking you from receiving your total breakthrough from the Lord, but that too has to come down!

I found out one of the reasons why some of us experience storms in life is the simple fact that Satan has a peak into our future. Think about it, if Satan didn't know about the Lord's plan for our lives, do you think that we would have to suffer?" Absolutely not! Satan only messes with those who he knows are a total threat to his kingdom. If you are no threat to Satan's kingdom then you need to check your salvation, or this may mean that Satan has you right where he wants you. But every trial we face in life will push us one step closer into victory.

Every trial you may have in life, just consider it a major opportunity to elevate to a higher dimension in God and into your next level of ministry. For eyes have not seen, neither have ears heard the good things that God has in store for you. Watch Goliath be defeated before your eyes. For your struggle is over; and get excited because this is your day for total victory!

THE ENEMY EXPOSED

You shall know them by their fruits.

Matthew 7:16

We are our biggest enemy—that is the flesh. A lot of times we need to rebuke the enemy out of our own self before we try to rebuke him out of others. This is a question that you need to really ask yourself: "Is the enemy really after me or is the enemy really in me? Many times it is not the actual enemy bothering you, but it is the *In-a-Me* that keeps you bound. It's this flesh that keeps many people bound from receiving all that God is willing to give. If we can get past this flesh, God can be seen in our lives. A lot of times we are rebuking the enemy out of other people, but what each one of us should evaluate and ask ourselves is this: "Is the enemy that I have been talking about and accusing, is he really in me?

It is okay to recognize the enemy and put him back where he belongs, we must truly decide if it really is the enemy or if it our own self that is doing something. A lot of times we blame the devil for things that we know we could have done better. This is why fasting and prayer is very important. Going back to the first chapter of this book, I have spoken about prayer and fasting. These are key principles to break free from the works of the enemy. The flesh is always wanting to do is own thing, always wanting with its selfish desires; however, from the flesh doing its own thing, from that, sin abounds. All sins bring curses, accordingly, if a person continues to live in sin. However, Jesus served as a curse for us all. He died so that we can lay our sins aside knowing that he paid the price for it, and to seek after righteousness. There is good news in Jesus dying for us, and the good news is this, "Christ hath redeemed us from the curse of the law, being made a curse for us: for it is written, cursed is every one that hangeth on a tree" (Galatians 3:13, KJV).

Not only does sin bring a separation from God, but sin can also lead to curses and eventually death. God made it clear in his Word in Joshua chapter 7 that accursed things and objects have a major effect on why people can't defeat the enemy from out of their life. God instructed Joshua to warn the Israelites to destroy every accursed object from among them; and because the Israelites brought accursed objects into their home, God allowed their enemies to defeat them.

If Jesus had not come, curses could not be broken; for sin was birth forth through the disobedience of Adam and Eve. Yet, God sent down his Son, Jesus— His only begotten Son—to cover the sins of the world. Jesus endured excruciating pain so that your children and mine can be free from every evil curse of Satan. Every generational curse that was over your family can be broken through the shed blood of Jesus.

There were many battles that the Israelites could have won, but because of the many accursed objects that they had in their midst, they were constantly defeated. But Jesus loves every one of us that he came to serve as a curse for us all! Let us know that Jesus took our every curse away when he died on the cross; and because of the events that took place on Calvary, no one has to endure the same pain, sickness, hatred, and abuse that their family had to encounter in the past. For the curse stops here!

Will you allow the curse of the enemy to continue to flow active throughout every generation after generation of your family's life? Will you allow the enemy to terrorize you and your family any longer? Don't you be like the children of Israel that wandered around in fear for this is your season to walk out in faith!

God gave the children of Israel biblical principles to follow that could have brought them to their promised land a whole lot sooner, but somehow, fear, disbelief, and rebellion set in, which literally caused them to wander in the wilderness a whole lot longer than usual. What was so important for the Israelites to hold on to their objects that God disapproved of? They were accustomed to their possessions that the possessions they had literally possessed them. Their objects then created a soul-tie between the two of them that they found it very difficult to let go. The Israelites wanted to serve God and hold on to their cursed objects at the same time, but God disapproved of that.

When a person becomes adapted to something for a long period of time they will sometimes find it a struggle to let that thing go. The following passage I will like to share with you shows the many things that can keep us bound from receiving the blessings that God promised to give. At times we are not wandering in the wilderness because of a particular sin that we have committed, but sometimes we find ourselves wandering in the wilderness because of sinful objects that we have in our midst. I will now like to share a couple of them with you:

TATTOOS EXPOSED

One thing I will like to speak about in particular is the curse of a tattoo. I know what some of you are thinking. "What does having *tattoo* have to do with being cursed?" Well, let's see what the Word of the Lord has to say:

> Ye shall not make any cuttings in your flesh for the dead, nor print any marks upon you: I am the Lord.
>
> Leviticus 19:28 (KJV)

So we see here in Leviticus that this is a mandate from God, not from me. However, God gives us many principles that we are to follow so that we will keep living a curse-free life. When dealing with tattoos, we must recognize the negative sides of them all.

Many of the Sorcerers of our time pass on their powers or demons through a tattoo on the body of a disciple; then, the disciple that has been given the tattoo forms a bond between them and their Sorcerer. The Sorcerer then controls their disciple's ability to achieve, and the disciple feels that he cannot make it without his Sorcerer.

Many persons get tattoos with names of people based on a relationship with that person. Some people get tattoos based on a relationship with a mother, a father, a sister, a brother, a lover, or a friend. But these are a few questions that a lot of these people ponder at times, "Why can't I succeed?" "Why does it seem as if the same routine is taking place day in and day out?" "Why can't I get *Johnny* off my mind?" The reason is this simple fact that you can't succeed in life nor get *Johnny out of your mind* is because *Johnny* has been attached to your skin and the same problems that *Johnny* had, has been passed down to you. You must realize that demons are transferable! There is not only one way that demons can transfer, but there are a numerous of ways that demons can be transferred. Whenever there is an opening somewhere that will allow demons access to come in. But we must be alert of the enemy, and we must be highly cautious to not engage in any of his evil activities. If you are not certain about getting a tattoo and the effects that it will have in the long run, your best bet will be to not get one at all. And you must always remember, *anything done without faith is sin* (Romans 4:23).

Other spirits and cursed objects include: Ouija board games, Dungeon and Dragons, magic 8 ball (prediction ball), dream catchers, tarot cards, good-luck dolls, good-luck charms, skeleton head jewelry, some wind chimes, and crystals.

Some people who follow certain strange religions pray over their products before they are sold to others. Many of these products that many people call fabulous works of art are nothing more than works of Satan in disguise. However, I find that some of these objects may bring curses. Some of the products that you have in your possession may just so happen to be a part of a demonic origin. "Do you know what you have in your midst? It's now time that you separate the ungodly from the Godly! It's time that you destroy every satanic object from among your presence!

When God sets you free from Egypt, don't bring the things that are in Egypt along with you.

In one incident a few years ago, a young girl happened to visit my church. I was around the age of eight at the time; I did not know much about cursed objects nor did I have much knowledge of demons. The young girl was around the age of seventeen. She proceeded into the church doors dressed like the usual members, with her nice Sunday attire on, with her hair fixed just right, with a gorgeous smile on her face; but it was something that was different about this girl from the rest of the people in the church. As I took a quick glance at her from the head on down, I could sense an evil presence or that something was demonic about her. This young girl happened to be wearing a moon necklace, seemingly to look like a demonic origin was attached to it; she also had the weirdest looking chain that was attached to her leg, but the only thing that was barely covering the chain was the cloths that she had on. Later, before the benediction, the time had arrived to take communion. Everybody began to reach for the communion bowl to participate in the holy ritual; thereafter, as we began the Lord's supper, the young girl couldn't find a way to keep it down in her system. Why was there such a struggle in the Lord's supper staying in her body, because the demons that was within her, knew that their time hand ended.

THE BLOOD PREVAILS!

After being saved for some time now, I realize that nothing can stand up to the blood of Jesus. Every now and then a painful situation will emerge; but when it does, we can apply the blood of Jesus to stand against it. The blood of Jesus will stand in the way of every weapon that the enemy brings. However, we must employ the blood of Jesus into our everyday life. When the blood of Jesus is applied to our life, everything that is bad around us has no other choice but to leave. For there is power in the blood! We can rely on Jesus' blood to receive healing, deliverance, restoration, and freedom. Every weapon we find the enemy throwing at us, we can stand in full assurance that Jesus blood will move his weapons out of the way. Thank you Jesus for your blood!

Meanwhile, once communion was finally over, it was during the benediction when the devil had decided that he was going to show up. "Is there anybody that needs to be saved? Does anybody need prayer? Then, come on down to the altar, don't let nothing or no one hold you back" uttered the assistant pastor.

After God had touched the young girl's heart, she decided to go to the altar for prayer. But while the assistant pastor and intercessors began to pray, the most outrageous sound that I have ever heard came from the young girl's mouth. A sound soared through the air that sounded like a whisper; then, later the sound started to escalate to a little soft moan. As the intercessors began to pray the more, the young girl's voice began to resemble a sheep's sound. *Baa! Baa! Baa!* was the sound. Right then and there, it dawned on me that this girl was possessed by a demon.

As the church starting praying, we were further instructed to pray in the Holy Ghost. After everyone knew that it was a demon and as the demons knew that we recognized who they were, the demons began to scream louder and louder. The demons inside of the girl did not want to come out. I could actually here the demons belting out "Leave me alone!" The demons began to speak out sounding as a full figured masculine man with a very deep voice.

During the process of the deliverance, one of the ministers from my church began to snatch off every piece of satanic jewelry that the girl was wearing. I did not quite understand at that time why the minister was taking the jewelry off, but now I know. When the enemy left this girl, his possessions had to leave along with him.

We must know that if a person is seeking true deliverance he or she can no longer hold on to the devil's things, they are going to have to let one of them go. The devil has many believing that if they have an object with them that it will give them supernatural power; but the only true source of power that I know of is the power of the Holy Ghost. The Holy Ghost is powerful to destroy all of Satan's works. Satanic objects worn by a person on in possession of a person does not bring them power but rather many curses—thus making it extremely hard for them to break free.

The young girl that was demon possessed was invited to church by her teacher. Later on throughout the service the teacher had the privilege to speak. The teacher revealed to the church that her student was practicing witchcraft in school with other young colleagues. The teacher happened to be a born again believer of the Gospel; and the young girl wanted to know more about Jesus, so she insisted that she come to church with her teacher to learn about Jesus and his plan for her life. The teacher knew of the demons that her student had in her. She knew that the demons were trying to destroy this young girl's life, and if she did not get help immediately, they were going to try to kill her. The teacher did not want to take her student to a mega church to get deliverance, because she figured that a mega church was too large and that the pastor of the church already had a lot on their plate dealing with their members. The teacher figured that bringing her student to a smaller congregation was a lot easier for the pastor to recognize this demon-possessed individual.

The deliverance process took a bit of fighting, but eventually the young girl broke totally free from her contract with witchcraft and with the devil. And right now the once demon-possessed young girl is totally on fire for God.

SATANIC NAMES EXPOSED

There are more than a zillion names for a person to think of before a baby is born, then when the baby is born, the name that he or she receives will follow them for the rest of their life. There are a huge source of good names and there are a huge source of bad names; however, let us deal with some of the bad names for a second.

We have to be extra careful with choosing our children's name. Without even knowing, we can be naming our children names that are rooted from the devil. However, false religions love to name their children after gods and famous ancestors; and immediately when they name their children after gods and famous ancestors, a soul tie is created. Some people love to name their child after a famous basketball player, baseball player, football player, soccer player, singer, actress, or other well-known person. I can't speak for no one else, but as for me I want to receive the name that Jesus promised to give me when he returns.

Names are an extreme importance to God. We can find that in Genesis 17:5 and Genesis 32:28 that God changed two individuals' names. The first name that

God changed was Abram to Abraham, and he changed the name of Jacob to Israel (Genesis 17:5 and 32:28). There were a few more other people in the Bible that God has changed the name of. Why did he change their names? Whenever God changed and individual's name in the Bible, he changed it because he saw what was greater in that person. In the book of Genesis, it was not too long after Abram obeyed the voice of God that his name was changed into Abraham.

> Neither shall thy name anymore be called Abram, but thy name shall be Abraham; for a father of many nations have I made thee.
>
> Genesis 17:5

> And he said, Thy name shall be called no more Jacob, but Israel: for as a prince hast thou power with God and with men, and hast prevailed.
>
> Genesis 32:28

Also in the book of Revelation, God promised that he would give each *overcomer* a white stone, and in the stone a new name is written, "Which no man knoweth saving he that receiveth it" (Revelation 2:17). In Revelation 3, God also promised this, "And I will write upon him the name of my God, and the name of the city of my God, which is new Jerusalem, which cometh down out of heaven from my God: and I will write upon him my new name" (Revelation 3:12).

So as we see in these two chapters of Revelation those have significant meanings. If I asked one-hundred students in a class to define their names for homework and tell me what it means when they come back to school, each student will be able to do that. Names mean a lot to God, and should mean a lot to us; but I have a question that I will like to ask "Do you know what your name means?"

You have to realize that all names are not always good names when a demon is involved. A lot of times people wonder why their children are acting a certain way out of the norm and are doing certain things, well let me ask you a question, "What do you call them?" A lot of parents call their children nicknames that are out of this world, and to the parents they think that the names are really cute, but when their children grow up and begin to do what they have been called all along, the parents later regret it. For example, if you choose the name "Crazy" as your child's nickname, don't be surprised if they start acting crazy. If you choose the name "Weed-Weed" as your child's nickname, don't be surprised if your child starts smoking weed. However, we have to be very careful what we name our children and what we name ourselves. A lot of people are speaking words of death over their children, and it stops their children's ability to achieve and to be successful.

Do not get mad at your child and tell them, "You act just like your daddy!" Don't tell your children, "Your daddy was nothing, and you are going to be nothing!" Your child is still your seed, and you do not want to destroy your seed with negative words of failure. Instead of speaking negative things over your children, tell this, "You are somebody! You look just like a teacher! You look just like a preacher! You look just like a doctor!"

Know that you have the power to name things what you want them to be; for there is power in your words!

Each one of us has the power to decree a thing, and it shall be established! So this means we have to speak the right things out of our mouth, and we have to highly realize that whatever we call ourselves or say about ourselves we will actually become that thing in which was spoken.

Another name that really stuck with me in writing this book is "Little Nut." Sometimes people wonder why their son "Little Nut" is acting completely out of disobedience and that is simply because of the demon that has been attached to the name. The guy who was named *Nut*; goes in on an interview, and the first thing the manager asks him when he gets there is this, "What is your name?" Once Little-Nut tells the manager his name, the manger then comes to the conclusion that Little-Nut will not be able to accomplish the work that the job is requiring because of his name; and if his name is Little Nut, then, if I give him this job, I wonder if he will act a little nut on the job.

A lot of times when I ask a person their name, they will give me their nickname; then I say to them, "no that is what people call you, but what is your name?" Very rarely will you find a name that sounds too much like a nickname to be a person's actual name, but it's possible. Does a name determine who you are as an individual? Absolutely not! However, I do feel that what you say about yourself does have a major effect on the person you will become. I heard someone say, that it is not what you are called that affects your life, but what you respond to. When you call on Jesus how does he respond? He responds by coming through for you. There is power in the name of Jesus!

Not only does this segment of this chapter refer to a person's name, but this section also refers to the power of spoken word. One of the major reasons why people go through painful situations in life is simply because of their mouth—the power of word. Every individual must take the initiative to realize that the mouth can be a carrier of life, or it can be a carrier of death. If you are speaking words of death, change them now! You have to choose your words wisely and be very careful of what you are thinking, because words and thoughts have a major part to do with how you live your life. Choose this day to start speaking life! Speak faith-filled words into the atmosphere; and unclutter your mouth from all negative words and fill it with the word of God. Just because you may have been called a crazy name all the way from birth, does not mean that you have to accept it. Someone may have called you a loser or a nobody, but that is not your name; for Jesus changed your name and your identity the moment you accepted him in.

> If it acts like a duck, quacks like a duck, it is a duck!

Remember our thoughts become our words, our words become our actions, and our actions determine our destiny. Where do you want to end up a few years from now? What business do you want to open? What goal do you want to achieve? Then don't be afraid to speak life! See yourself in the home of your dreams; see yourself being a highly successful business owner; and don't be afraid to declare it out of your mouth! Stand with your head in the air and say, I will succeed! I do have a multimillionaire mind-set!

STRANGE OBJECTS EXPOSED

Some people believe that every object that is in their home is okay to have. Many say to themselves "There is no way I can get rid of this object; I just know that one day this object is going to make me rich!" Meanwhile, years have passed and they are still saying the same thing "Nope can't let this object go, It's going to one day make me rich!"

God has great blessing for his people, but he cannot give them to us while we are still holding on to the cursed objects of the enemy. There are some people who are now in a bad condition hanging on to things from the past. Satan has to let God's people go, and it is time that you as a child of God take back everything that the devil has stolen from you! For this is your season of blessings, but don't nearly think that holding on to Satan's objects will gain you victory, it won't. But if you want Satan to let your possessions go, you are going to have to give him back his. Everything that Satan has only last for a temporarily basis, but what Jesus has to offer last for all eternity.

God has given me the authority by his Spirit to warn every person about demons that can be in our homes without us even being aware. Have you ever wondered why your children act the way they act, and why the relationship between you and them can't ever grow into an area of trust? Well, let me ask you a question, "What toys are your children playing with? What games are they playing? What are your children watching on television?"

However, these are questions that I am concerned about when I see so many children walking in disobedience. Children are very quick learners, and at times, they will hear something or watch something and immediately begin to define what it is that is being brought to them. Children are like a sponge; they will absorb everything that is in their midst.

What is your possessions worth? Are your possessions worth living in bondage? Are your possessions worth living in fear? Are your possessions worth living with a dreadful curse for many, many years? Often, it is easy to tell a person's way of living by the many things they have in their home. At times I will catch a glimpse of people with books in their home, and when I notice a lot of books, my first thoughts that come to mind are that the person loves to read. However, a lot of people that I have encountered constantly complain about them having nightmares, but when I go to their home all I notice is demonic figures of dragons, snakes, skeleton heads, and black cats. But some of the reasons why many people go through depressed stages in life are because of objects. Some objects will hinder a person from enjoying life. Then, after awhile, the person will become bound to their object where they will find it very difficult to get rid of. On the other hand, some objects follow a person from house to house but as the person moves their objects along with them, the demons that are connected to the objects move as well.

You may be reading this book, and maybe you are the one who likes to run from your problem; but, this is the time that you stand in your problem's face and say "I will not keep you around any longer!" You will continue to endure the same problems over and over again if you do not expose the cursed object and get rid of it from your home.

One type of art I like in particular is African art. Not one time did I know that I was opening a big door for satanic-invasion the minute I realized that some of the objects that I liked had curses connected to them. In some stores throughout the world today, they sell African pieces of art with women carrying baskets on their head; a lot of the women are either seen barefooted or just simply naked. However, when I notice these figurines in people's homes, a lot of times the person who has them are financially struggling either living from paycheck to paycheck or are borrowing from Peter to pay Paul. But I wonder how can a person expect to have enough money in their purse and in their wallet, when their home is full of objects of homeless men and women carrying baskets on their head, and trying to make ends meet? This is a poverty demon that is in the home, and it must be completely destroyed!

Some cursed objects can lead to sickness, depression, oppression, confusion, fear, torment, pain, agony, generational curses, rebellion, witchcraft, perversion, discomfort and so many other things; however, God has given us the full directions to take in breaking free from the many snares of the enemy but all we have to do is follow them step by step. The first step in the process of being set free is to destroy every object that belongs to Satan. Once you get rid of Satan's objects you will experience so much joy, peace, and an overflow of blessings coming into your life.

But not only does satanic objects open wide gates for the acceptance of demons, but movies and TV shows open wide gates for the acceptance of demons as well. In the times ahead Satan will try to control the minds of people in many ways. However some of his way is by widely introduces his drafted out hobby to the world through movies, cartoons, toys, and even clothings. Some of the things that were very shocking were the movies and television shows, and these really have shocked my attention. Many of them feature occultist themes such as: friendly Smurfs, Bart Simpson, Beavis and Butthead, and others set people up for an invitation from the enemy. But knowing the enemy's tactics, one thing we will find is that he likes to sugar-coat things up to the best of his ability. Not all demons appear to be scary and not all demons have long vans sticking out of their mouth, but many of them can appear as alluring people and action heroes such as: Santa Clause & the Elves taking people away from the real meaning of Christmas and focusing it on Santa instead of Jesus. Also you have Casper the friendly Ghost, the Tooth Fairy, The Smurfs, and so many others. Demons come in all different shapes, forms, and fashions needless to say; God has given his children power over them all. The more you spend time in Gods' presence, will be the more your eyes will become open to recognize the seducing plots of the enemy when he comes.

Satan will try his best to make something bad appear good (this is how he lures his bait); whatever tries to take the place of God is what Satan will try to use. During Christmas and Easter season it is Satan's greatest plan to take people's attention of off the one who is the reason for both of these seasons Satan allures little children into believing that Santa Claus is the reason why Christmas exists, then as the child grows, each year they focus more and more on buying gifts and Santa Claus than they do on the real meaning of Christmas—Jesus Christ. Then, Satan wants to allure the little ones a little more, so he introduces them to the Easter Bunny, and his beautiful eggs; meanwhile, as a child is highly amazed at the Easter Bunny's color, they miss the real reason why Easter really exists.

We cannot give Satan any worship—for that is what he wants, but we are to give all glory and all worship unto God. Satan desires to be our god; Satan wants to keep us to focus on Christmas gifts for Christmas than focusing on the real and true Christmas gift that we can ever have, which is everlasting life.

Satan's schemes are very real, but I am here as an ambassador of Christ to expose some of Satan's schemes to you. We cannot be ignorant of Satan's devices, and we must highly place him under our feet; for we are victorious through our Lord and Savior Jesus Christ!

PORNOGRAPHIC MUSIC EXPOSED

Now, let us discuss the issue of pornography. Most individuals know of someone struggling with this issue, and many of them deal with it on a day to day basis themselves. Very seldom do we hear pastors preach on this stronghold addiction of the enemy, and why is that, because many of them need to be set free themselves. This is a strong hold that is running rapidly throughout the world, from sex tapes to sex pictures, but what we must realize is that at some point in life each one of us has experienced a time when our sexual organs have began to rise. For God made us all beings with sexual organs; however, Satan wants us to give in to our sexual organs' desire and start to do exactly what are sexual organs are desiring; but when we are not married and have sex, our bodies become defiled before God. We must realize that we are the temple of the Holy Spirit; and we must also realize that the Holy Spirit does not dwell where sin is. It is very imperative that we clean our bodies completely from sin, so that the Holy Spirit can dwell freely at his will.

Satan has been hiding peaked over in a corner for quite sometime, and he's been afraid to let the world see the real him. Satan does not want the saints of God to expose his mess, but I am not worried about exposing Satan's mess because he is under my feet. I truly believe that if many spirits are exposed, lots of people will get delivered. The reason why many individuals are not being delivered is because the pastors are not teaching them true deliverance. You cannot get something that you don't know about. It's time for deliverance, healing, and freedom to take place in the church! Can we give God the Privilege to move by his Spirit the way that he wants to move! God desires to deliver each and every one who is looking for deliverance.

If you are seeking for deliverance, seek no more because God is here to deliver you; but he is waiting on you to open yourself up to divine deliverance allowing him to come in. Will you give God the opportunity to deliver you from every evil work of Satan? Will you allow the Holy Spirit to live inside of you so that the enemy can no longer move in?

There are many forms of pornography and so many other things leading to it. One of a major form that I will like to discuss now that is dealing in pornography is the subject of music. What does music have to do with pornography? Music has a lot to do with pornography; however, did you know that spirits can also be transferred by a particular song? Yes everyone there are pornographic songs out there that are killing the minds of individuals! We need to be very careful with the different kinds of music that we are allowing our spirit-man to feed on. Many seducing songs in this generation are perverted and diluting our young ones into perverted relationships, and many of these songs talk on the three-letter word. Now come on, you know what the three-letter word is! The three letter word is *sex*. Many listen to these songs and all they can talk about when the song is over is this "When am I going to get with this person or have sex with that person?" and before they know it, the doors for the enemy have already been opened.

In heaven, Satan was the ruler over music, and today he tries his very best to take back what he has already lost. Satan is out to pervert the music, pervert the land, and pervert our youth with his evil seed, but we as warriors of Christ have to go get our land, go get our community, go get our music, and go get our youth back from the enemy! This is the time for the true Christians to rule and to rise in full authority!

Rock music is another demonic form of music that many people highly overlook; but rock music is very powerful. In times past around society many witches did incantations and rituals which placed demonic spirits on every record of rock music; however, the person playing the music couldn't hear the demons, but as the person slowly rewound the tape they could hear the demon's and their message very clear. A lot of people I had the privilege to speak with about hardcore rap music, revealed that a lot of the words that they heard in a song were a whole lot different as they played the song backwards.

Also, the person who is playing these satanic songs causes for demons to arrive to afflict them and anyone else who is listening to the music being played, then, the one who is being afflicted and tormented later on becomes depressed, oppressed, and a lot of times, fearful. However, satanic music is a number one cause of suicide in the world today. What is the purpose of a person listening to satanic music? It gives Satan the opportunity to control their mind. Yes my brothers and my sisters, Satan wants to control your mind! But how does he do that, by getting you to hear something that is interesting to your ears, then you say, "This is my jam!" but do not know the demons that are behind them. One of the reasons why people are on the street visualizing things out of nowhere is because Satan has clogged up their thinking capacity by the music they have allowed into their minds. You must realize that people will actually become what they listen to. This is why it is very important that we guard every word we are allowing into our mind, because if we listen to trash, we too will become trash. Trash is meant to be thrown into the garbage not into your mind.

Have you ever noticed that drug dealers, abusers, and sex predators all listen to the music that most describes them? It might sound funny, but it's true! However, you must know that whatever words you say out of your mouth whether they are in music form or just simply words in general, they will have a good or bad effect to the many things that come into your life. If you want to have blessings flowing into your life, listen to music that speaks of blessings. If you want to experience healing in your life, listen to songs that speak on healing.

Music is most common among the younger generation; they constantly listen to music, from CD players, the radio, iPods, MP3 players, iPhones, the internet, and television. Many young teens, kids, and toddlers know a huge amount of songs that are being played today; but I find it a major problem that *Little-Sally* is quoting lyrics from drug dealer's music singing about getting drunk and having sex—it shouldn't be! This is why we must guard what our children are listening to, what they are watching, and what they are getting involved in. Satan is out to seduce our young ones by the music that is being played but we as saints of God must take a stand!

At a church that I used to attend, there was a man that came to visit. Later throughout the service the man was asked to give a brief testimony of what happened to one of his nephews a few years ago. The man's nephew was around the age of seventeen at the time. The nephew was very much approaching the stage of peer pressure. He was the type to hang with his friends and listen to hardcore rap music. So, one day, the young man came home from his outing with his friends and brought with him a tape that he had borrowed from one of his friends; however, the young man's mother was a Christian who disallowed anything that was not of God to enter into her home. The young man knew how his mother would react so he tried to figure out a way that he could get the tape into the house without his mother seeing it.

As the young man slowly tiptoed through the front door of his home, he then slowly peeped to his bedroom to place the rap tape on the shelf, but little did he know that his mother was watching him the whole time out of the corner of her eyes. Meanwhile, as the young man made it to his bedroom and shut the door to find relief, his mother screamed, "Boy, what did you bring into this home! Give it to me now!"

Because the young man was obedient to his mother's rules and regulations, he quickly handed his mother the tape. But as he began to place the tape in his mother's hands, the tape magically jumped out of his hands and then out of nowhere began to spin on the floor. As the rap tape began to spin on the ground, it was not minutes later when out of nowhere the tape began to slither like a snake.

The young man and his mother had never experienced anything like that before; and they were dreadfully frightened. Because the two of them didn't know what to do in what they saw, they ran towards the front door to get help. The mother made it out the house alright, but as her son was trying to get out behind her, he was tripped by an unseen force. The force had a grip on him that it tried to literally suck the very life out of him.

Meanwhile, the mother ran next door as her son was still in the house to get help from her neighbors, but little did she know that her neighbors were born again believers. The mother was trying to explain to the neighbors what had happened and because they had a strong gift of discernment, they knew exactly what was going on and that it was nothing natural, but spiritual.

Later on, the young man's mother along with the neighbors went back to their home to pray, anointing the walls and pleading the blood of Jesus; however, before they even approached the inside of the house, everything appeared back to normal. This experience really startled the mother's son to the point that he destroyed every demonic record that he had.

Sometime it will take a person to experience something horrific like this in order to get their attention to destroy every satanic tape from out of their presence. The devil doesn't care what he uses and who he uses to get to the minds of individuals. The devil is after our youth starting from birth, all the way up to an adult;

and children do not focus on school and the books like they used to because the songs are telling them that it is okay for them to drop out of school and become a weed-head; young kids who are in elementary want to do exactly what they see the artists on TV doing, but now is the time that we bridge the gap!

There is a problem when children know every word of a hardcore rap song but can't even say their ABCs. You will be shocked to know all of the kids that know songs about drugs, sex, and violence more than someone who is twice their age; and trust me when I tell you, the kids know exactly what the song is saying!

Studied research shows that many kids that are rebellious have listened to music leading to a rebellious nature. However, in 1 Samuel 16:23 we will find that Saul was disobedient to God, and from his disobedience to God, an evil spirit was placed on him. But God used one who could drive the demon away so He called forth David, who was a Psalmist as well as a musician. David's music was so much anointed that as he began to play his instrument, the demons that were in Saul had no other choice but to leave.

> And it came to pass, when the evil spirit from God was upon Saul, that David took an harp, and played with his hand: so Saul was refreshed, and was well, and the evil spirits departed from him"
>
> 1 Samuel 16:23, KJV

When the even was come, they brought unto Him many that were possessed with devils:

and He cast out the spirits with his word, and healed all that were sick."

Matthew 8:16 KJV

I find it strange how someone can hear a song about killing someone and then out of nowhere get a certain urge to kill? Demonic spirits are being transferred through the media of music, on the internet, on the radio, and on the television.

Have you ever listened to a song and you didn't understand the words of it, but you danced and grooved to the song because you liked the particular beat? This is exactly how Satan lures many into his traps. Satan lures his bait by using someone's favorite artist to promote his kingdom; Satan has his plans all laid out; he figures, "If I can use this rap artist in his rapping, maybe I can work a deal with him that if he brings more souls to me through his rapping, I will keep money flowing in his pockets, and after I use him to bring me glory and allow him to enjoy life with his money, fancy cars, fancy houses, and ladies for awhile, I will destroy him in the process." We have to be very watchful of the enemy. Satan desires for us to worship him by the many devices that he is using, but we have to outsmart him by using some of the devices that we have of our own against him.

What Satan does not know is that, while he is using a rapper to win a person to worship him, Jesus will eventually turn that rappers heart another way, and the soul that the rapper won over to Satan, will be the same soul that gives their life to Jesus by hearing their favorite rapper singing the Gospel—the true message! For God can change man's heart the way that he wants for he is in total control.

A lot of the songs that are out now go straight over some of our heads. Satan wants to lure us with the beat of a song that we do not pay close attention to the words. Satan has even had the nerve to take the music into the church. He even tries to stop us from worshipping God—our Savior and the Creator of everything—to worshipping him. Satan told Jesus in the wilderness that he would give him kingdoms of the world if only he would bow down and worship him; but little did Satan know that Jesus already owned everything that he was trying to give him.

Satan wants to clog people's minds to the point that if it's not what people want to hear, they can't receive it. However, we must realize that God desires our worship and that we must are bowing down to him. Every time that we sin we bow down to Satan. For the enemies works are destroyed through our obedience to God. We cannot give Satan the privilege to dilute our music and our minds with his garbage. It's time that we take our music back and return it to its truest form. It's time for the Christian singers to take the stage and sing the Word of God! For it is the anointing that destroys the yoke of the enemy, not this demonic music they have out now trying to produce more sales and trying to get more money into their banking account.

Also, some of the Gospel singers that are out now need to place the Word into their songs. Some of the Gospel songs that I hear do not mention anything about the Word or about Jesus; for we must realize that there is power in the Word of God and in the name of Jesus!

If you want to know where to send all of the homosexuals, lesbians, adulterers, fornicators, sex predators, drug-addicts, warlocks, witches, and fortune-tellers then send them right into the choir. I am not trying to be rude, but the truth is the truth! We cannot go around the truth; this is exactly why many churches are torn apart and the members are doing any and everything they want to do is because there is no order. The pastor refuses to discuss issues that have been overlooked for many, many years because they do not want to lose their members; because if they lose members, they lose money. But now it is time that we call a sin the way it really is! It is time that we call a demon by its real name and stop substituting its name to make it look good.

In the Bible, in the book of Matthew, Jesus asks the demon inside of the man his name and the demon responds, "Legion!" which means that there were many demons within the man.

God is looking for our true worship. God is looking for us to worship him out of a sincere heart; however, when we worship God we must know that we cannot worship him where there is mess around; we have to first get rid of the mess, then we can worship God. Also we must realize that we cannot continue to keep straddling the fence and expect for God to bless us. Once we get rid of the lying, gossiping, hating, backbiting, cheating, and stealing, then real worship can flow freely into our lives and through our church.

SATANIC CLOTHING

All satanic objects and satanic clothing must be completely removed from your presence.

> The graven images of their god shall ye burn with fire: thou shalt not desire the silver or gold that is on them, nor take it unto thee, lest thou be snared therein: for it is an abomination to the Lord thy God. Neither shalt thou bring an abomination into thine house, lest thou be a cursed thing like it: but thou shalt utterly detest it, and thou shalt utterly abhor it; for it is a cursed thing.
>
> Deuteronomy 7:25–26

> What I say then? That the idols is anything, or that which is offered in a sacrifice to idols is anything? But I say, that the things which the Gentiles sacrifice, they sacrifice to devils, and not to God: and I would not that ye should have fellowship with devils?
>
> 1 Corinthians 10:19–20

I am a very huge fanatic when it comes to fashionable clothing. You can find me wearing some of the latest trends in shirts, jeans, and shoes; however, there are certain things that I will not wear. I remember there was a time when I went shopping, and I just couldn't wait to get in the store to try on the clothes. My eyes bucked when I realized that a lot of the clothes in the store were half off or a buy one get one free special, and in my mind I was like wow! And boy, can I tell you that the clothes were extremely amazing! When I reached for the tag labeled on the products in the store, I realized that a lot of them were labeled as a satanic-trend. Many shirts I focused my attention on had skeleton heads on them, while other shirts had scorpions, death-angel wings, pythons, dragons, gods, guns, bullets, weed trees, black cats, spider webs, and other demonic symbols labeled on them. I thought that I could get away with not purchasing the shirts and jeans and to focus my attention on other things in the store, but boy can I tell you that the shoes, the hats, the belts, and the socks all had satanic symbols on them. I couldn't believe what I was seeing!

Lots of people are being seduced by the enemy, but someone has to stand up and bridge the gap, so it might as well be you. If the devil can't get a person any other way, he will try to get them to purchase the type of clothing accessories that they love to wear, but we have to utterly *detest* them as the Word of God says.

This is a question that everyone reading this book should ask themselves, Do I make clothes, or do clothes make me? Constantly it is indicated in the Scriptures for us to change our filthy garment and to put on holy garments. The Word of the Lord also declares for us to put on the garment of praise for the spirit of heaviness. Also, in the book of Zechariah, Joshua, one of the high priests, had on filthy garments when he stood before the angel of the Lord, and the angel that approached him spoke to those who were standing near to take away from Joshua his filthy garments, because God was going to cloth him with a change of raiment (Zechariah 3:3–4, KJV).

Just as God had a change of raiment for Joshua to wear, we must know that if he tells us to get rid of something he tells us because he has something even better to give. However, Jesus explains in the book of Matthew, that no one puts a new cloth unto an old garment because it will make the garment even worse; what this is saying is that, you cannot keep asking God to cloth you with his garments and keep holding on to the garments of the enemy as well. We must realize that new things always replaces the old; however, we need to stop holding onto the old and get ourselves ready for the new that God is about to give us.

> No man putteth a piece of new cloth unto an old garment, for that which is put in to fill it up taketh from the garment, and the rent is made worse. Neither do men put new wine into old bottles: else the bottles break, and the wine runneth out, and the bottles perish: but they put new wine into new bottles and both are preserved.
>
> Matthew 9:16–17 (KJV)

I know many are thinking that I am saying that it is what you wear that you are judged by, that is not what I am saying, nor am I the one to judge. There is only one judge and that is God. It is not the outside that makes a person, it is the content of the heart that determines them. I truly believe that what you put on will have a major effect a lot of things that you are dealing with on a daily basis. Just as leeches cannot live without attaching themselves to something demons are quit the same. Leeches need something to leech off of in order to manipulate an individual; and whatever sales the most is what the enemy will use as a trap to lure his bait. Many of the clothing that some of us wear are highly crafted with demons. Some people that manufacture such products have blessed their products to make the people wearing them succeed or curse them in keeping them in bondage.

> Do you make the cloths or does cloths make you?

Each one must realize that demonic clothing can make a person sick, confused, fearful, depressed, oppressed, and bound. For example, some people who are wearing shirts with death-angel wings, skeleton heads, or snakes have experienced lots of physical pain in their bodies. Every time they go to the doctor, the doctor cannot find anything wrong, and this is because it is not physical, but spiritual. A lot of the people who experience different pains in their body do not realize that the demons that are connected to the clothing have entered into them. Demons leech onto cloths just to leech onto a person that buys them.

This is the time that you discern what you have in your possession that is not right and destroy it. You may be trying to hold on to things from the past, but now is the time to let them all go! God has far greater things in-store for you, but He cannot give you the greater while you are still carrying onto old waste of the enemy. As I have said earlier, waste is meant to be thrown into the trash; so stop holding onto the garbage of the enemy and put it where it belongs, throw it in the trash!

> And the Lord said unto Joshua, Get thee up; wherefore liest thou thus upon thy face? Israel hath sinned, and they have also transgressed my covenant which I commanded them: for they have even taken of the accursed thing, and have also stolen, and dissembled also, and they have it even among their own stuff. Therefore the children of Israel could not stand before their enemies, because they were accursed: neither will I be with you any more, except ye destroy the accursed from among you. Up, sanctify the people, and say, Sanctify yourselves against tomorrow: for thus saith the Lord God of Israel, There is an accursed thing in the midst of thee, O Israel: thou canst not stand before thine enemies, until ye take away the accursed thing from among you.
>
> Joshua 7:10–13 (KJV)

There are many bound by the enemy because of cursed objects. Have you ever wondered why a person is sick, depressed, and delayed from walking into their blessings? There are too many weights somewhere. You must be the one to decide, "Should I hold on to this nice piece of art that I know is a demonic sign of the enemy and that will keep me bound, or will I get rid of it?" One of the reasons why the Israelites couldn't find a way in defeating their enemies was because they wanted to hold onto their pieces of art that God disapproved of. But in order for us to receive the blessings that the Lord has promised to give us, we have to make him first in our lives, and we must know that he will not share his glory with any man; for God says, "Either your idols or Me!"

There are even some relationships that many of you need to cut off; *for how can two walk together accept they agree*. And if someone is not agreeing with the same thing that you agreeing with, then this is a good time to cut them off. What is holding you back from moving into your full potential in Christ?

David in the Bible was a true praiser, and I can imagine him saying to himself "I need to break free from bondage. These clothes that I have on are holding me back, so let me dance right out of them!" So if you know that objects are keeping you locked up in prison from enjoying life, then you need to shake them off. I guarantee you that once the objects are destroyed from out of your life there will be so much joy and security knowing that the enemy has finally left your life for good. Whatever area you were struggling in before reading this book, now that you know how to defeat the devil in your life and know that he can no longer approach you with the same temptations that he has brought your way in the past, you have gained the victory for the enemy has been exposed and you can now live your best life!

DESTROYING THE YOKE OF THE ENEMY

Take my yoke upon you, and learn of me; for I
am meek and lowly in heart: and ye shall find
rest unto your souls. For my yoke is easy, and
my burden is light.

Matthew 11:29 (KJV)

L et's look at the word, "Yoke," for a second. What
is a yoke? According to Merriam Webster's
Dictionary, a "yoke" is "something that is placed or
tied on an animal's neck in two equal portions so that
it can be led." As this one definition of a yoke refers
to an animal and how they are led by their neck, this
definition also refers to humans. However, the problem
that many people around society today have is that they

have been tied down to the wrong yoke, and because of that many of them are going in the wrong direction.

A yoke can also be a frame fitted to a person's shoulders to carry a load in two equal portions. So we see here from this definition that a yoke can either be good or it can be bad, but it is all based on whose yoke that you have around you.

Jesus says in this in the Scriptures, "Take my yoke upon you, and learn of me; for I am meek and lowly in heart: and ye shall find rest unto your souls" (Matthew 11:29–30). What type of rest is this that Jesus is willing to give? He is willing to give us a rest that will sustain our lives for tomorrow. Jesus is willing to give us rest from every storm that we are in. Jesus wants to give you and I rest from sickness, disease, pain, frustration, confusion, fear, doubt, worry, and the only way that he can do that is we must first allow him to have complete control. Jesus wants to give us rest, but he cannot give us rest while we are always on the go. A lot of us want the Lord to speak to us, but he has always been speaking. We have been talking too much and too loudly to even hear him speak.

Jesus wants to lead us in the right direction. He wants us to take on the yoke of him. It will require us to be completely joined to him and then led by his spirit—the Holy Spirit. When I agreed to place the yoke of the Lord around me, I realized that it was no longer I, but him who dwells in me.

> According to my earnest expectation and my hope, that in nothing I shall be ashamed, but with all boldness, as always, so now also Christ

shall be magnified in my body, whether it be by
life, or death.

Philippians 1:20 (KJV)

Now unto him that is able to do exceeding
abundantly above all that we ask or think,
according to the power that worketh in us,
Unto him be glory in the church by Christ Jesus
throughout all ages, world without end. Amen.

Ephesians 3:20–21 (KJV)

This is a question that I want to ask you: *Who are you being controlled by?*

Have you ever wondered why you were going in a certain direction, and when you wanted to do your own thing you couldn't? You need to realize who is controlling you. Are you being controlled by the devil or are you being controlled by God? Regardless of who is controllin you, you will become a spitting image of them. To fully understand control, a person must realize that there are two types: Good Control and Bad Control. Good Control is looking out for a person's safety as well as the requirements that the person needs in order to achieve. Bad Control, on the other hand, is always intended to manipulate and intimidate an individual to the point that it causes them, the victim, to breakdown spiritually and even to the point of death.

When I was born into the world I realized that I was no longer of my own. When I came into the full knowledge of Jesus Christ, I found out that I was purchased with a price the very second that I told the

Lord, "Yes." However, when something is purchased the purchaser can do whatever they want to do with their product, but the problem with many in society today is that they have been purchased by the wrong purchaser and instead of them being driven by the Holy Spirit, they are being driven closer to hell by the devil.

With me accepting Jesus into my life, he promised that he would send his spirit, to guide me and lead me into all truth. But many times we fail to realize that we will have to obey someone some way or another, and we only have two decisions to make; we can choose God, who gives us life, or we can choose the devil, which brings death.

Does it make you angry when you buy something and somebody tries to tell you what to do with your product? This has to say a lot about us. We are all a product of someone. However, whomever a person is being controlled by, they will still have to bow to the name of Jesus; that is for all men! Because at the name of Jesus, every knee shall bow, and every tongue shall confess that he is Lord! Those individuals who made Jesus the Lord of their life must realize that he is in complete control. There is no time that you are in control; for God is the Potter and you are the clay. Allow God to lead you by his spirit and being led by his Spirit is the best way to go. God will not lead his children in the wrong direction nor will he put his children to shame; however, those who are being led by the devil are always going in the wrong direction and are always being put to shame; for Satan was a liar from the very beginning, and if he tells his followers to go in a certain direction he is lying to them, and going his way will lead them to destruction if they keep following in his tracks.

When a person is demonically possessed, it is not he or she who is acting out of control; it is the demonic spirits that are inside of them. However, when a person is not walking in total alignment to the Word of God the way they should, they give Satan legal access to possess them. Once Satan is invited in to a person's life, he then will believes that he can do what he wants, when he wants, and how he wants to do it. Satan wants to be in complete control even if that gives him the authority to control the minds of every last individual on planet earth.

You must let the devil know that you have complete authority over him. You must take control of your mind, over your thoughts, and over your words and not allow the devil to take control over you. The devil wants to keep you in bondage, but the good news is this: "For ye have not received the spirit of bondage again to fear; but ye have received the spirit of adoption, whereby we cry, Abba, Father" (Romans 8:15 KJV).

Another thing that Satan wants you to do is meditate on things that are contrary to holiness. The Apostle Paul tells us this, "Stand fast therefore in the liberty wherewith Christ hath made us free, and be not entangled again with the yoke of bondage" (Galatians 5:1 KJV).

If there is anything more shameful than seeing someone bound in the prison of the enemy is to see that same individual drive themselves back to the prison after Jesus has set them free. For the Word of the Lord declares, "Whom the Son sets free are free indeed." Now, if Jesus sets us free, why do we constantly go back to the things that Jesus died on the cross for? I hear people say at times, "I want to be delivered from smoking or drinking but I just like what I do!" "I really want to be delivered from cursing and fighting, but let me just tell them off just one last time!" But remember *faith without works is dead.*

We can have abundance of faith in our talk, but how can we have true faith if it does not become a walk? We must know on a daily basis that God will lead us in the right direction. We must believe that God will deliver us from every bad habit that we have that is not of him; then, we have to put some action behind our faith talk.

The objective of the enemy is to form an illusion in the minds of the believers to have them believing that what he says is actually true; meanwhile, after the believers quoted words like: *I can*, the words have drastically changed to *I can't*. However, this subject reminds me of the story in the Bible about the lady who suffered with an issue of blood for twelve long years. This lady didn't sit at home murmuring and complaining, but she put forth some works with her faith. She said, "If I may touch the helm of Jesus garment I know I'll be made whole." And despite all the gossipers in the crowd, this lady received what she was seeking years.

Faith is just like a plant; when a plant is placed in the ground it cannot grow unless it is properly watered, fertilized, and has the proper amount of sunlight; however, when it comes to our faith, we cannot grow productively in faith if fertilization, and watering is not maintained daily. From a Spiritual perspective, the way we water our faith is by staying in the Word of God— the spoken word of God. Everything that exists in this universe would have not been; the world was framed by the spoken word of God. When everything else fails we can depend on the Word of God as a sure guarantee—as a sure promise— that what he says will come to pass.

> Now a certain woman had a flow of blood for twelve years, and had suffered many things from many physicians. She had spent all that she had and was no better, but rather grew worse. When she heard about Jesus, she came behind Him in the crowd and touched His garment. For she said, "If only I may touch His cloths, I shall be made well." Immediately the fountain of her blood was dried up, and she felt in her body that she was healed of her affliction. And Jesus, immediately knowing in Himself that power had gone out of Him, turned around in the crowd and said, "Who touched My cloths?" But His disciples said to Him, "ye see the multitude thronging You, and You say, 'who touched me?'" And He looked around to see her who had done this thing. But the woman, fearing and trembling, knowing what had happened to her, came and fell down before Him and told Him the truth. And He said to her, "Daughter your faith has made you well. Go in peace, and be healed of your affliction."
>
> Mark 5:25–34 (KJV)

For we walk by faith, not by sight.

2 Corinthians 5:7 (KJV)

When we have faith we don't mind moving ourselves out of the way and allow the Holy Spirit to be in total control. Every believer must have faith knowing that God will supply all of their need. You can have everything you need, but it's all according to your faith. Luke 17:6, KJV: "And the Lord said, 'If ye had faith as a grain of mustard seed, ye might say unto this sycamine tree, Be thou plucked up by the root, and be thou planted in the sea; and it should obey you.'" When it comes to deliverance, a person must take a step of faith by saying I'm ready to receive my deliverance and the activation of faith opens the door for deliverance to take place in their life.

I wrote a song that says, 'Faith is the Key if you want to be free." Yes, faith is the key if you want to be free, but once you get the key you have to be willing to unlock the door. Don't just have the keys and not use them; for you must know and always remember that faith unlocks the door to your future.

This is another excuse that people love to use, "It's Just Too Hard!" Sometimes people use the word *hard* to justify why we are still doing what we are doing. God will not make anything just too hard for you. He will never put more on you that what you are able to bear; however, we can bring hard situations on ourselves. Don't get me wrong, we will have to go through some things in life that we do not want to go through but only for a season; however, the storms we go through in life are being used as tools to help build up our faith.

If you are seeking deliverance confess your faults, not to me, but to the Lord; for he said that he is faithful and just to forgive your sins. "But what good is confession without repentance?" Confessing is a powerful way to defeat the devil. So start confessing your faults and watch God destroy what the enemy thought that he had planned.

> If we confess our sins, He is faithful and just to forgive us of our sins and to cleanse us from all unrighteousness. If we say that we have not sinned, we make Him a liar, and His word is not in us.
>
> 1 John 1:9–10 (KJV)

Another powerful tool to use as a weapon against the enemy is that of faith. The Word says that we are to fight the good fight of faith; however, before we fight we must make sure that we have on the proper attire. There is no way for a soldier to prepare himself for war without having on his proper garments. The proper clothing for battle are as followed: "Stand therefore, having your loins girt about with the *truth*, and having on the *breastplate of righteousness*. And your *feet shod with the preparation of the gospel of peace*. Above all, take the *shield of faith*, wherewith ye shall be able to quench all fiery darts of the wicked. And take the *helmet of Salvation*, and the *sword of the Spirit, which is the word of God: Praying always with all prayer and supplication in the Spirit*, and watching thereunto with all perseverance and supplication for all saints" (Ephesians 6:14–18, KJV).

If we wear these proper garments for war, there is no way that we can be defeated. There are a whole lot of methods that we can use to overcome the devil, but not only do we have methods, Satan has them as well, and I will share a couple of his methods in the next few chapters of this book. However, some of Satan's methods are as varied of the person that he is dealing with. In the book of Genesis, Satan came to Eve in the disguise of a deadly serpent. How did Satan know how to trick Eve into disobeying God, he knew exactly what was pleasing to her eye.

Satan will try to use our desires to trick us into disobeying God. Satan knows what makes us happy, what makes us sad, what makes us afraid. He even knows the right button to push, but he does not want to be exposed in seducing his victim, so he covers himself with a wide load of different disguises. Satan knows how to put on a form of godliness; however, he denies the power thereof. Satan knows how to roll around on the floor at church thinking that no one will notice the real him. Have you ever watched a scary movie and when the movie first came on it didn't show you the ghost, monster, or murderer right then and there, but it started to reveal slowly who they were in the middle or right at the end of the movie? However, Satan's disguises are somewhat the same. Satan will hide from his bait in sheep's clothing for a little while, then, later on he will turn into the big black wolf and destroy his bait. More times now than ever, Satan is revealing himself more boldly because he knows that his time is winding up.

> But if our gospel be hid, it is hid to them that are lost: in whom the god of this world hath blinded the minds of them, which believe not, lest the light of the glorious gospel of Christ, who is the image of God, should shine unto them… For God, who commanded the light to shine out of darkness, hath shined in our hearts, to give the light of the knowledge of the glory of God in the face of Jesus Christ… We are troubled on every side, yet not distressed; we are perplexed, but not forsaken; cast down, but not destroyed.
>
> 2 Corinthians 4:3–4, 6, and 8–9 (KJV)

DROP THE HABIT ON THE GROUND AND IT WILL BREAK!

A bound individual can't break free from the enemy's chains until he or she makes up in their mind that they are willing to change. We have to use our methods that God has commissioned every believer to fight with. We should get in our attack mode and be able to discern when Satan is trying to make his attack. Many people ask this question: "Lord if I am your child, then why am I being attacked?"

God never said that the enemy wouldn't come; as a matter of fact, he lets us know in his Word that the enemy will come. However, he also lets us know that when the enemy does come, the Spirit of the Lord will lift up a standard against him. God also lets us know that we should always walk by his spirit; for the Holy Spirit is our alarm against the enemy who warns us when the enemy is trying to come in. Many have gone through danger simply because they have refused to hear the alarm of God. For the devil is like a roaring lion seeking whom he may devour, and this is why we must keep our mind fully occupied in the word of the Lord.

I hear people say all of the time that an idle mind is the devil's workshop. This is why it is highly imperative that you write the vision that God downloaded into your mind and fully walk in it with no delay. It is not too late for you to start dreaming. God may have downloaded a vision into your mind of a business that he wants for you to open; this is your season to walk in it! Do not allow the enemy to steal your vision, because if he can steal your vision, he can steal your passion and your joy. Also, in working your vision you are to fully work the Word. If you allow God to come into your vision, he will allow everything to work in your favor as it comes to pass.

The enemy may have lied to you by saying you can't complete anything, and everything you put your hands to do will never prosper, but the devil is a liar! God told me to tell you that you can do all things through him because he strengthens you! God will never start something in you and then not finish it. However, many of you may say this, "If God started a work in me, why don't I feel like nothing has changed?" You must realize that some work can be delayed through disobedience, but that does not mean that the work has been completely denied.

Some of you reading this book may be fully obedient and submitted to God, but you may feel like some things in your life have never changed, just know that the work has already been started in you, but you will gradually change little by little. If you were fully complete and perfect you would not have to depend on anyone. But each step you take in your Christian walk puts you at another level to learn and brings you closer to your victory!

LIVING WITH A CURSE

The Lord has given me a revelation on Satan's many tricks, schemes, and lies. If we take a glimpse in the Bible at the book of Genesis to Revelation we can clearly see how big Satan grew. From the book of Genesis, Satan presented himself in the form of a snake that deceived Adam and Eve; and in the middle of the Bible, Satan tempted Jesus in the wilderness and others constantly. However, as we read from the new testaments to the last book of the Bible, Revelation, we can clearly see a big transformation in how Satan grew from a snake to a dragon. Sometime in the Bible in the middle of it all Satan was being fed.

A lot of times we try to nurture a demon by telling it how cute it is, dress it up, and play with it; but when the demon begins to get stronger and much larger, we then regret doing everything we have done in causing it to grow. A major issue that is going on now is homosexuality. Many are struggling with this issue

Byron Walker

from the young as well as the old. Now it seems that this demon is much stronger than ever.

Little Jimmy wants to play with Barbie-dolls rather than play sports. And instead of Little Johnny playing video games, he wants to play with mommies' makeup and lipstick. Also a lot of kids are not getting attention from their parents, so they decide to experiment with other things, and a lot of them are beginning to play house. You know the fairytale that we all use to play when we were younger when we act like we were married and had children. Little John wants to play house, but little John doesn't have a girl to play house with, that will act as his wife and the only source that he has is Little Jimmy; then, Little John plays husband, while Little Jimmy plays the wife.

Many have set in silence knowing that something crazy was going on with their son or with their daughter but because of ignorance they said, "They will grow out of it one day!" Then, years progressed and the demon got larger and larger because no one said anything to put a stop to it, and before they knew it, their child went on to adapt to the way they were feeling.

Let me ask you a question: Will you continue to allow the Devil to operate in your family's life? Will you continue to allow the devil to operate in your life? You and members of your family can be delivered today!

Now I will like to discuss more about this issue of homosexuality. Homosexuality is sexual interest in or contact with members of the same sex. Female Homosexuals are called lesbians, after the Greek island of *Lesbos* where in ancient times the poet Sappho wrote

148

accounts of this type of relationship. Among psychologists and other experts, much controversy exists as to whether homosexuality is a mental illness. Some people believe that homosexuals who are well-adjusted to their way of life cannot be justifiably classified as mentally-ill, others believe that homosexuality is deviant behavior and therefore represents a mental disturbance.

Most investigators, however, believe that homosexuality probably results from such environmental factors as emotional conflicts in child-parent relationships during adolescence. Homosexuality is more common among males than females. Surveys and investigations regarding sexual behavior in the United States indicate that a substantial number of persons, both male and female, have had homosexual encounters sometime in their lives, usually in their youth. Only a small percentage of these persons, however go on to adopt homosexuality as a consistent sexual pattern.

"What does the Word of God have to say on homosexual behavior?"

"Thou shalt not lie with mankind, as with womankind: it is abomination. Neither shalt thou lie with any beast to defile thyself therewith: neither shall any woman stand before a beast to lie down thereto: it is confusion"

(Leviticus 18:22–23, KJV).

"Wherefore God also gave them up to uncleanness through the lusts of their own hearts, to dishonour their own bodies between themselves: Who changed the truth of *God* into a lie, and worshipped and served the creature more than the Creator, who is blessed for ever. Amen'. For this cause God gave them up unto vile affections: for even their women did change the natural use into that which is against nature: And likewise also the men, leaving the natural use of the woman, burned in their lust one toward another; men with men working that which is unseemly, and receiving in themselves that recompence of their error which was meet. And even as they did not like to retain God in their knowledge, God gave them over to a reprobate mind, to do those things which are not convenient; Being filled with all unrighteousness, fornication, wickedness, covetousness, maliciousness; full of envy, murder, debate, deceit, malignity; whispers, Backbiters, haters of God, despiteful, proud, boasters, inventors, of evil things, disobedient to parents, Without understanding, covenant breakers, without natural affection, implacable, unmerciful: who knowing the judgment of God, that they which commit such things are worthy of death, not only do the same, but have pleasure in them that do them"

(Romans 1:24–32, KJV).

Most persons dealing in homosexuality have been rejected and on most cases they have been physically abused. Truth reveals that a lot of homosexuals only adopted homosexuality as a way of being accepted. If someone is being rejected the only way for them to find acceptance is to get in where they fit in.

Jesus died for the homosexuals as well as for anybody else. If you are homosexual, the good news is that you can find deliverance today! Maybe you are saying homosexuality is not one of my issues, well whatever your issue is, Jesus died for you because he loves you and he loves you so much that he is willing to deliver you! Homosexuality is a strong hold and it can be broken! All throughout life I have come across people who told me that they were dealing with this issue, and they really didn't know how to break free from it. They told me that they have prayed and prayed and still couldn't find a way in being free, well I asked, if they liked what they did, and many of times the answer was yes.

One thing we have to realize and that is for anybody to be free from any seduction, you must first make up in your mind to want to be free. God can deliver, but you are going to have to want it bad enough. Deliverance can be yours today! Another person told me that whatever you crave the most, you will want more of it. I strongly believe that those who crave more of righteousness and pleasing God receive a major outpour of God's glory in their lives. God fills those who are thirsty and hungry for him.

The answer is not that when you have prayed for deliverance that God didn't hear you, the answer in many cases is that you have prayed and prayed for deliverance to take place, but while you were praying maybe you should have added in your prayer, Lord fill me with an outpour of your spirit!

I believe that there are those who are desperately in need of God to the point that if they don't have him they will starve from not receiving what He has to give. God's desire was to send redemption to mankind by sending his Son Jesus to carry the burdens of every sin on the cross. Jesus died so that you could be free. He died so that you wouldn't have to experience lost or so that you wouldn't be lost.

You may be saying this, "homosexuality is not something that I just accepted but God made me this way." This is not the way God made you. God made you beautiful in his image and in his likeness. You have not been made to be a homosexual, but you have been made for purpose to be all that God wants for you to be. Jesus loves you! But my question to you is: are you willing to make a change? I know it might not be an easy thing to do but with Jesus on your side he will help you to defeat homosexuality to the fullest degree.

If you are reading this book and have an issue that you are struggling with, today can be your day of deliverance! If you truly want to be free, you can be free and delivered today! If you are really sincere about being delivered then say this prayer with me:

> Lord I boldly confess to you my sins; I know that I haven't always done what I was supposed to, but I refuse to do what I used to do. Now Lord I open myself up to divine deliverance, have your way in my life now! Set me free from every sin, every curse, and every temptation. Lord you said in Your Word that whosoever should call on your name shall be saved. And Lord I thank You for my safety now. Lord I thank You now for my complete deliverance.

Lord by faith I believe that I am set free from
the enemy's chains; I give you all the praise, the
honor, and the glory and I seal this prayer now
in Jesus name I pray. Amen.

If you have just prayed this prayer, watch God do
what you need him to do. Secondly, take out the time to
praise God for your deliverance. Trust, believe, and be
confident about the fact that God has heard your prayer
and put the rest of your problems in his hands. Spend
much time in the Word on a daily basis and continue to
pray with much fasting included, because some things
can only come out through fasting and prayer.

> Who hath delivered us from the power of
> darkness, and hath translated us into the
> kingdom of His dear Son. In whom we have
> redemption through his blood, even the
> forgiveness of sins.
>
> Colossians 1:13–14 (KJV)

LIVING WITH A CURSE: THE TRANSFERENCE OF SPIRITS

> Take heed and beware of covetousness: for a
> man's life consisted not in the abundance of the
> things which he possesseth.
>
> Luke 12:15 (KJV)

> For ye suffer, if a man brings you into bondage,
> if a man devour you, if a man take of you, if a

man exalt himself, if a man smite you on the
face.

2 Corinthians 11:20 (KJV)

People suffer in bondage because they choose to.
However, Jesus came to set us free from bondage, and
because of Him suffering on the cross, we don't have
to live in bondage ever again. Greek word for *bondage*
is *katadouloo*, which means "utter enslavement." Those
who are in bondage cannot think for themselves, their
master will do all of their thinking for them. Many
people on the other hand have become a slave to the
enemy. Many have made the work of Satan their first
priorities, not even realizing that when they work for
him they become one of his slaves.

You cannot be one of Satan's slaves. You need to make
Jesus the master of your life. However, the difference
between serving Satan and serving God is that, Satan
works all of his slaves to death, but God on the other
hand, gets the glory out of the work that His child does
and with them doing His work, they will reap a harvest
of blessings. Also, every believer must realize that when
you are doing the work of Satan immediately you
become open to receive a transference of evil spirits; and
spirits can be transferred in a numerous type of ways.
One way that a spirit can be transferred is through a
family member; other ways that spirits can be easily
transferred is through a friend, a spouse, associates,
television, internet, movies, books, toys, clothes. Some
people would least expect that evil spirits can transfer
from these particular things and people, but they can.

Another way that people will least expect for evil spirits to be transferred is through the mouth. Yes evil spirits can be transferred through the mouth. The mouth is a little part of the human body but it does a whole lot of physical damage. This is why we have to be very careful of the words that come out of our mouth. The Word of God lets us know that the words we speak out of our mouth can produce life of they can produce death. The words that come from out of our mouth drops out seeds and every time we say the same words over and over again those seeds begin to grow. Many times people wonder why there are so many giants in their life. You may feel this same way saying to yourself, "If it's not one thing it's another!" Well, how many seeds did you plant? Things grow were seeds has been planted. Do you want a good seed or do you want a bad seed to grow? It's time that you remove the good seed from the bad ones. The power is in your words. Decree and declare that your seed will be blessed! Decree and declare that your child's seed will be blessed! There will be no more bad seeds sprouting up; for it is the time that you reverse the curse of the enemy!

I have encountered people suffering with many different illnesses and not only them, but members in their family have or are suffering with the same illness. Whenever a person goes to the doctor for a physical checkup the first thing the doctor checks in the process is their family history. The doctor will try to get to the deep root of the problem by asking questions. The doctor may ask them, "Well did your mother or father deal with the same illness?" And from that person's response, the doctor can properly diagnose what is going on in this person's body. The whole purpose of a doctor asking questions about their patient's family is to see what is in the bloodline of their patient's history. But if we cancel the works of Satan from the bloodline, there is no way that his works can travel to the next generation.

FAMILIAR SPIRITS LEVITICUS 19:31

If you take out the letters *-ily* from "family" and add the letters *-iliar*, what do you get? As you see you will get the word *familiar*. Familiar spirits can dwell in the midst of a family for many, many years until someone recognizes and puts a stop to them.

Have you ever heard a person say that their loved one that is dead has come back to visit them? Some say that their deceased loved one has passed on but their spirit still lingers around comforting them throughout the day. Does this sound familiar to you? However, these are all familiar spirits that need to be exposed and that need to be bound by the Holy Spirit, by the Word of God, and by the blood of Jesus.

God's word is very accurate where a family spirit is involved. In Leviticus 20:27, people who are seeking after ungodly spirits for guidance are actually breaking the first commandment. God is a jealous God, and he will not share his glory with another.

Saul began his search by seeking for an answer. So Saul figured that, because God wasn't speaking to him that he will seek guidance from a witch of Endor; however, Saul was entertaining a familiar spirit.

> And when Saul saw the host of the Philistines, he was afraid, and his heart greatly trembled. And when Saul enquired of the Lord, the Lord answered him not, neither by dreams, nor by Urim nor by prophets. Then said Saul unto his servants, Seek me a woman that hath a familiar spirit, that I may go to her, and enquire of her. And his servants said to him, Behold, there is a woman that hath a familiar spirit at Endor. And Saul disguised himself, and put on other raiment, and he went, and two men with him, and they came to the woman by night and he said, I pray thee, divine unto me by the familiar spirit, and bring me him up, whom I shall name unto thee. And the woman said unto him, Behold, thou happen to thee for this thing. Then said the woman, Who shall I bring up unto thee? And he said, Bring me up Samuel. And when the woman saw Samuel, she cried with a loud voice: and the woman spake to Saul, saying, Why hast thou deceived me? For thou knowest what Saul hath done, how he hath cut off those that have familiar spirits, and the wizards, out of the land: wherefore then layest thou a snare for my life, to cause me to die? And Saul sware to her by the Lord, saying, As the Lord liveth, there shall no punishment thou art Saul. And the king said unto her, Be not afraid: for what sawest thou? And the woman said unto Saul, I saw gods ascending out of the earth. And he said unto her, What form is he

of? And she said, An old man cometh up; and he is covered with a mantle. And Saul perceived that it was Samuel, and he stooped with his face to the ground, and bowed himself. And Samuel said to Saul, Why hast thou disquieted me, to bring me up? And Saul answered, I am sore distressed; for the Philistines make war against me, and God is departed from me, and answereth me no more, neither by prophets, nor by dreams: therefore I have called thee, that thou mayest make known unto me what I shall do. Then said Samuel, Wherefore then dost thou ask of me, seeing the Lord is departed from thee and is become thine enemy? And the Lord hath rent the kingdom out of thine hand, and given it to thy neighbor, even to David: Because thou obeyed not the voice of the Lord, nor executedst his fierce wrath upon Amalek, therefore hath the Lord done this thing unto thee this day. Moreover the Lord will also deliver Israel with thee into the hand of the Philistines.

1 Samuel 28:5–19 (KJV)

Saul was seeking for an answer to his many problems, but because of his disobedience to God, he was drawn further away from God. Saul made a gigantic mistake when he went after familiar spirits rather than hearing and obeying God the first time. Saul received demonic guidance which was very wrong.

You must realize that when you are seeking guidance from demonic advisors rather than seeking the Lord, you are headed for a fall. Many seek after guidance from witches, warlocks, sorcerers, and even fortune tellers to try to find solutions to their many problems. Some even take it a bit further and turn to people that say they have a close communication with the dead. But what each person must realize is that these are all evil spirits. Saul, on the other hand, entertained many demonic spirits, which later led him down the road to death and eternal separation from God as we will find in 1 Chronicles 10:13–14.

When we accept Jesus into our lives his spirit guides us and leads us into all truth, and because of the bloodline of Jesus, we have been given total permission to communicate with the Father because he now lives inside of us. When we sin our communication with the Father becomes blocked. God specifically expresses this in the Scriptures when he says your sins have separated you from the love of God. But because Saul disobeyed God, not only did his sins separate him from communicating with God, and God communicating with him; his sins had also separated him from the love of God. But the good news is that God is a merciful God who is willing to receive each and every one of us again if we repent to him and if we do it in his Son Jesus' name out of a sincere heart. God's line is always opened, his arms are stretched out wide, and he is never too busy to come see about you if you are ready to return back to him. God hears a sinner's prayer, and he is merciful enough to receive them again. And when a person repents out of a true heart that is what turns the line back on between them and God the Father.

Will you hear what the Father has to say? Will you allow Jesus to live in you? Will you allow His Holy Spirit to lead you into all truth? God wants to speak to you; lend him your ear today! He wants to give you something that will last for all eternity. But why do people seek guidance from others when they too need guidance? I don't understand! How can the blind, deaf, and dumb lead the blind, deaf, and dumb? You are not blind, deaf, nor dumb because you now have the Holy Spirit as your guide.

> And when they shall say unto you, Seek unto them that have familiar spirits, and unto wizards that peep and that mutter: Should not a people seek unto their God? For the living to the dead?
>
> Isaiah 8:19 (KJV)

Remember, Satan can put on a form that will become a splitting image of you, and if you are not careful to hear the voice of God, you will give in to his artificial appearance. Satan appears in all different shapes, forms, and fashions; however, he can also appear as an angel of light. Satan is out to deceive many by coming to them with a form of God. Many are falling into his traps because they will rather believe a lie rather than the truth. Many who have started out strong in the faith have gone on to establish a new type of doctrine that suites them as well as their sin. You all need to know that sin is sin; there is no other way in describing the sins of man.

But though we, or an angel from heaven, preach any other gospel unto you than that which we have preached unto you, let him be accursed.

Galatians 1:8 (KJV)

And the soul that turneth after such as have familiar spirits, and after wizards, to go a whoring after them, I will even set my face against that soul, and I will cut him off from among his people.

Leviticus 20:6 (KJV)

When thou art come into the land, which the Lord thy God giveth thee, thou shalt not learn to do after the abominations of those nations. There shall not be found among you anyone that maketh his son or his daughter to pass through the fire, or that useth divination, or an observer of times, or an enchanter, or a witch, Or a charmer, or a consulter with familiar spirits, or a wizard, or a necromancer. For all that do these things are an abomination unto the Lord: and because of these abominations the Lord thy God doth drive them out from before thee. Thou shalt be perfect with the Lord thy God. For these nations, which thou shalt possess, hearkened unto observers of times, and unto diviners; but as for thee, the Lord thy God hath not suffered thee so to do.

Deuteronomy 18:9–14

And it came to pass, as we went to prayer, a
certain damsel possessed with a spirit of
divination met us, which brought her masters
much gain by sooth saying: The same followed
Paul and us, and cried, saying, These men are
the servants of the most high God, which shew
unto us the way of salvation. And this did she
many days. But Paul, being grieved, turned and
said to the spirit, I command thee in the name
of Jesus Christ to come out of her. And he came
out the same hour.

Acts 16:16–18 (KJV)

*When the devil sees you does he see a Reflection of Jesus,
or does he see a reflection of himself?* Whenever you have
an encounter with a demon you must let that demon
know that you mean business. You cannot show any
sympathy to the devil nor can you allow him to defeat
you in any kind of way, but you must rebuke him in Jesus
name knowing you have total authority over him. You
will not be defeated by the devil because God made you
a victor and not a victim! It is not a buy one get one free
special. The devil will not play fair and neither should
we. But what we must do is out— trick the enemy in
his—own game. We need to stop throwing pity parties
with the devil and put him where he belongs, and that
is, under our feet!

Don't you think it's about time for you to stop
playing games with the devil? As long as you continue to
think that the enemy is your friend you will constantly
be disappointed. If you have gone from one abusive
relationship to the next, it only means a familiar spirit

that has followed you, and you need to put that spirit under your feet.

Familiar spirits are demonic agents who have a specific assignment to draft as many weak individuals as they can into demonic contracts with them. Familiar spirits become well acquainted with the person whom they are dealing with. Familiar spirits must report back to their head master, which is Satan whose job is to find our areas of weakness, so that they can tell him everything he needs to know about a person. Familiar spirits know what a person likes, what they dislike. Familiar spirits know what makes a person happy, what makes them sad, and what make them even afraid, but God says that everything the enemy brings is only false evidence appearing real. Everything that Satan says is a lie—the truth is not in him—it never was and never will be. Whatever area we are weak in we cannot let the devil know that area of weakness. Even in our weakness God is there to give us strength and comfort; his strength is made perfect in our weakness.

> Then certain of the vagabond Jews, exorcists, took upon them to call over them which had evil spirit's the name of the Lord Jesus, saying, We adjure you by Jesus whom Paul preacheth. And there were seven sons of one Sce'-va, a Jew, and chief of the priests, which did so. And the evil spirit answered and said, Jesus I know, and Paul I know; but who are ye? And the man in whom the evil spirit was leaped on them, and overcame them, and prevailed against them,

so that they fled out of that house naked and wounded.

Acts 19:13–18 (KJV)

When the devil recognizes that you are a child of God, he will flee from you because he knows that your Father will arrive on the scene. The reason why the devil knew who Paul was when he first saw him was because Paul's life reflected Jesus. I have a question to ask, "*When the devil sees you does he see a reflection of Jesus, or does he see a reflection of himself?*"

Every person that is on this earth the devil has a different disguise to give to every last one of them; however, his schemes are all the same. The devil uses the same old outdated tricks constantly but periodically he will change his face. There are different demons assigned to a person by what they are accustomed to. Witches for instance, lure their bait by giving them what they want. Witches can present themselves to people as light; they can come to you dressed with the same cloths, walking the same walk, and even talking the same talk—that is Christian talk. Usually when a person thinks about a Witch, broomsticks, green face with a big bump on their nose, extremely long hair, big black hat, and a big black cape come to mind. However, witches are very pretty at times while they use their charming appearance to lure others into their traps.

WITCHCRAFT EXPOSED

It has been a myth for very long that witches go flying around the moon on broomsticks sprinkling their evil portions in the air, but those are all lies! But can you believe that witches do exist. Witches do not go flying around on broomsticks all day long, but many of them are in places where you would least expect. Some are operating in witchcraft sitting in the pulpit, carrying a title behind their name so that the title can disguise the real them. Yes it must be said! It's time for use to sweep witchcraft from out of our churches throughout the world.

Witchcraft, in historical, anthropological, religious, and mythological contexts, is the use of alleged supernatural or magical powers or spells. In early modern Christian Europe it was widely believed that witches were in league with the Devil and used their powers to harm people and property. The concept of witchcraft as harmful is normally treated as a cultural ideology, a means of explaining human misfortune by blaming it either on a supernatural entity or a known person in the community.

Since the midtwentieth century "bad" and "good" witchcraft are increasingly distinguished, the latter often involving healing. Witchcraft is all of the devil however, beliefs in witchcraft, and resulting witch-hunts, existed in many cultures worldwide and still exist in some today, mostly in Sub-Saharan Africa (e.g. the witch smellers in Bantu culture). Historically these beliefs were notable in Early Modern Europe of the fourteenth to eighteenth century, where witchcraft came to be seen as a vast diabolical conspiracy against Christianity and accusations of witchcraft led to large-scale witch-hunts, especially in Germanic Europe. The "witch-cult hypothesis," a controversial theory that

European witchcraft was a suppressed pagan religion, was popular in the nineteenth and twentieth centuries. Since the midtwentieth century Witchcraft has become the designation of a branch of neopaganism, specifically those Wicca traditions."

Is witchcraft among us today? Yes, witchcraft is among us today. Throughout the world and in many places today, witchcraft is widely seen. Witchcraft is widely recognized through manipulation, intimidation, and abuse. Witchcraft has a lot to do with why many are experiencing crazy things of today. A lot of it has to do with witchcraft. There is a reason to the crazy things that you are dealing with. There is a reason to why at times you find yourself not succeeding in life. There is a demonic force and right now it is time for it to be exposed! Now is the time that you gain your authority over the devil and let him know that there is no power that he can bring to you that will stop God's plan for your life!

In many instances witchcraft did occur in times pass and in many occasions. According to the New Standard Encyclopedia, "Witchcraft is the practice of magic, especially evil magic—called black magic or sorcery—by a person known as a witch. Witchcraft is also the supposed ability of certain witches to cause evil without performing any acts of magic. At one time the term, "witch" was applied to both men and women, but eventually the name was restricted almost exclusively to women. In Britain and America, a male witch is usually called a warlock, sometimes a sorcerer or wizard.

Witchcraft is going on rapidly throughout the world today, also did you know that rebellion is as a form of witchcraft? That is what 1 Samuel 15:23 says: "For rebellion is as the sin of witchcraft, and stubbornness is as iniquity and idolatry. Because thou hast rejected the word of the LORD, he hath also rejected thee from being king." This is when God took the anointing away from Saul. Saul was the one who went after vain things. A lot of people are practicing witchcraft today and not even knowing it. Those who are operating in rebellion are operating in witchcraft; that's what the Word of the Lord tells us. Whenever a person has total authority over you to the point that they control your every move, they are practicing Witchcraft—which is also a form of control. Whenever a person has the authority to tell you to live your life based on the way they want you to live, this is a form of Witchcraft. We are to live our lives to please God, not man; for God is the creator of the universe and over every human being that has ever existed. Whenever you are being controlled by someone other than God, they are operating in witchcraft. Now don't get it twisted, I am not talking about you being disobedient to authority, what I am saying is if someone is making you do something that is outside of the will of God, that is control and you need to break free from that! According to the New Standard Encyclopedia,

> The most common concept of a witch is that of a woman who exercises supernatural powers through the aid of the devil or evil spirits. A witch is generally believed to have the power to fly, to cast harmful spells, to disclose future or hidden matters, to transform herself, and to produce anything she wishes. Each witch is thought to

belong to a coven, a band of thirteen witches. The belief in witchcraft is both ancient and widespread. The ancient Egyptians believed in witchcraft.

(Funk & Wagner 266).

In Europe, The early Christian church soon identified witchcraft with heresy, and condemned its practices as survivals of pagan evil. After 1258, one of the duties of the inquisition was to suppress witchcraft. In 1484, Pope Innocent VIII issued a bull directing that witches be put to death. Persecution of witches was especially prevalent in England in the mid–1600. It is estimated that at least 150 supposed witches met with the devil on certain nights, called sabbaths or witches' sabbaths to reaffirm loyalty to him, mock Christianity, plan evil deeds, and revel until dawn. On sabbaths, the devil was reputed to conduct the Black Mass, a parody of the Christian Mass.

(Funk et al. 266).

The campaign against witchcraft spread to America, reaching its peak in Salem, Massachusetts. In 1692 several Salem girls began to behave peculiarly and to accuse persons of bewitching them. Fear of witchcraft spread, leading the governor to appoint a special court to try persons charged with witchcraft. One man was pressed to death with weights for refusing to plead either guilty or not guilty, and many others were jailed.

(Funk et al. 266).

In Western Culture, Witchcraft has had a revival in the second half of the twentieth century. Some of today's witches still claim to exercise supernatural power for evil through the aid of the devil or evil spirits. The majority, however, differ from traditional concept of the witch in two ways: they claim to obtain supernatural power from pagan deities not evil spirits; and they claim to use this power for good purposes not evil ones. This form of witchcraft has a number of followers in both Great Britain and the United States. Some meet regularly in covens for worship of their deities. Several groups maintain museums of witchcraft.

In Primitive Cultures, in many primitive societies, people attribute misfortune, disease, and death to supernatural means, such as witchcraft, when they cannot explain the trouble by natural means. In some societies witches may be either men or women; in others male witches or female witches predominate.

Attitudes toward witches vary from one society to another; so do attempts made to detect them and counteract their witchcraft. Many primitive societies have a tribal specialist, a shaman, or a witch doctor, whose job is to detect and overcome witchcraft, especially when it causes illness. He usually has a good knowledge of medicinal herbs and of his patients' personal problems, and his patients generally have complete confidence in his ability to cure. This background enables him to treat many ailments successfully. The person who acted in this capacity for American Indians was known as a medicine man.

Primitive witchcraft has negative aspects. In places where human hearts and other body parts are regarded as charms against witchcraft, people have been murdered to obtain them. Belief in witchcraft has often impeded the spread of modern medical treatment among primitive people. On the other hand, many anthropologists say that witchcraft beliefs serve a useful purpose, giving people a definite scapegoat— the witch-to blame for trouble. The procedures for countering witchcraft give people the feeling that they are doing something to combat misfortune, thus making misfortune easier to bear (Funk et al. 277).

Witchcraft has been around for many, many years. Witchcraft is mentioned in the Bible, and on numerous of occasions, God indicates in the Word that those dealing in witchcraft and sorcery will be in extreme danger of hell's fire.

Jezebel is a prime example of one who worked witchcraft from a global perspective. Jezebel was a lady who operated strongly in this spirit. She was also one who didn't obey. She wanted to do what she wanted to do and in certain instances her duty was to kill the men of God. Not only did Jezebel do evil works of Satan; but in the Book of Exodus, we will find that there were many in those days that were practicing witchcraft.

In the book of Exodus, God instructed Moses to lead the Egyptians out of Egypt; Moses thought to himself that he was not equip with what it was that he needed to lead the Children of Israel out of Egyptian bondage, but God told Moses that everything that he needed was already in his hands. However, Moses could not speak right but that did not put a stop to God using him. There were a lot of sorcerers in the land in those days that amazed many people with their witchcraft and their magic abilities; however, despite of Moses ability to speak the language of his brother, Aaron, and the Israelites, God still spoke to him; Moses still had the ability to hear and recognize the voice of the Lord.

Everything that God instructed Moses to do, Moses later instructed his brother Aaron to do. Meanwhile, Moses and his brother Aaron went in unto Pharaoh and they did so as the Lord commanded, and Aaron cast down his rod before Pharaoh and before his servants, and it became a snake. Later, Pharaoh called the wise men and the sorcerers and they did likewise, they cast down their rods and they all became snakes. But the thing that was so amazing was that as the sorcerers and magicians cast down their rods, Aaron's rod swallowed up their rods. As revealed in Exodus 4:1–31, what was so special about Aaron's rods from the rest of them was that God was in it, and you must highly realize that whatever God is in, he will make you prosper and Satan will have to back out. You cannot prosper with Satan being in the midst, but God is so awesome and all powerful that even if Satan is in the midst of his righteous people; he will allow them to rise over their problems even with Satan standing in the way. When the enemy comes in like a flood, the spirit of the Lord will lift up a standard against him. Witchcraft, sorcery, and voodoo are all worthless to the powerful blood of Jesus—for the blood prevails!

Not only did witchcraft exist in past times but there are a lot of witchcraft groups around the world today. A lot of these groups come together on special occasions having group meetings on the person who they are going to try to afflict. Many of the people dealing in this cult of witchcraft keep it a total secret from those not dealing in the cult. Many of the sisters that are in the cult of witchcraft portray to be of the truth, but they are nothing more than a deadly serpent in disguise. Many of these sisters you will find visiting churches throughout the world doing silent chants during the church service to try to afflict the pastor as well as the members. While the church service is going on and everybody is praising and worshipping God, these sisters sit way in the back of the service and highly observe the weak individuals from the strong ones, and of course, these witches' main target is to get to the weak individuals.

I have been in some services were the pastor would recognize that a witch was in the building and would command for the witch to leave. Many times while the witch or warlock was sitting in the church, they would silently do chants to try to weaken the ministry and prey on victims to use against their leaders.

This is the time to pray like never before because the enemy has begun to get bolder than ever. It is our duty as children of God to get even bolder. It is time that we stand our ground!

Do not allow anyone to pray over you whom God does not permit. If you are in church and your pastor is the person who is preaching for the hour, if he or she has not prayed over you themselves or instructed a person in the church to pray over you, then do not allow anyone to do so. Everybody that says they are a prophet does not necessarily mean that they are doing the work of a prophet or the work of the Lord. If you get caught on titles every time, you will be deceived. There are some people who have titles in the church that are nothing but witches and warlocks. Witches and warlocks are running rapidly in the church and if you are not in tuned to the spirit of God, you will fall into their tracks.

God tells us in the Word that *ye shall know them by their fruit.* This Scripture does not say that you shall know them by their title; for you must always remember, *Satan can present himself as an angel of light.* There are witches and warlocks who are hosting meetings throughout the world, and many of them are being held right around many of us. My prayer is that the spirit of God will arrest the witches and warlocks who withstand God's anointing as he did with Jannes and Jambres in the days of Moses (Exodus 7:11–22). My prayer is that Satan's powers be eradicated and that those operating in witchcraft break free and be filled with the Holy Ghost and with fire!

Witchcraft has no power over the Blood of Jesus. This is why placing the blood of Jesus in your life has major importance. No foe has power over the blood. Every spell and hex shall not pass through the bloodline of Jesus. Know that when the enemy sees the blood he has to flee. I challenge you to apply the blood of Jesus over every situation that you are in and watch the blood work on your behalf!

Witchcraft and magic work hand and hand; however, witchcraft is a higher level of magic in which it afflicts, tortures, or even curses its victim. Magic on the other hand, is the art that claims it controls natural forces directly by supernatural means. The word comes from "magi." In magic, think that if a person recites or rehearses certain words, or performs certain acts, in a set order, desired events are bound to occur. The formula of words, and sometimes the entire ritual, may be known as a spell, charm, rune, or incantation. Conjuring is another term for a magic ritual, especially if it is for summoning a demon or other spirit. The magic formula is often in verse form, and may be chanted or sung. Sometimes magic objects are used in ritual.

According to some beliefs, anyone can perform certain kinds of magic. However, magic may be practiced as a specialty by some individuals, known as magicians, wizards, witches, sorcerers, conjures, or diviners. In primitive societies, persons such as shamans, part-time religious leaders, and witch doctors, specialists in detecting and overcoming witchcraft, use both magical and non-magical procedures. However, all forms of magic and witchcraft are still sin.

People of modern cultures often believe in magic, and consult fortune tellers, wear good-luck charms, and avoid walking under ladders. Belief in magic is called superstition, especially when found in modern times. Superstition is a form of witchcraft. Throughout society today attractive looks are called "charms." Most fairy tales, myths, and folklore are woven around magic elements. Many times, when people are referring to love, they will refer to it as a "magic spell." There is a song in particular that says, "I put a spell on you, because you're mine!" This is a scheming and conniving form of witchcraft; getting a man or woman the wrong way by putting a spell on them to bring them to you then for them to be drawn to you themselves is a disaster waiting to happen. I think each person trying to get into a relationship should pray to God and tell him, "Lord if it's not you bringing this person to me then do not let them come." And don't you be the one to manipulate a person to you when they do not want to be with you, because when you do that you are getting your hand caught in a huge amount of fire. Do not allow the enemy to seduce you into witchcraft through manipulation and intimidation, and do not allow the spirit of Jezebel to be born into your life—for the spirit of Jezebel must die!

Whenever we think of magic traditionally, we think of black magic; but maybe, you did not know that there is also white magic. White magic some believe is beneficial, cures sickness, makes crops grow, and ensures success in all lines of endeavor, but the outcome of it is still sin. Black magic is called witchcraft or sorcery. It causes sickness, accidents, and death; the spoiling of crops; and drought, flood, and other misfortunes. Often the difference between black magic and white is in the point of view. A shaman makes white magic to ensure his tribe's victory in battle; but his work is black magic to the enemy whose warriors are killed and whose villages are raided.

We have to come to full agreement that witchcraft is very real! Satan's weapons are not just imaginary weapons that are formed, but they are very real indeed; however, God the Father, God the Son, and God the Holy Spirit are more powerful than all of Satan's weapons. Satan has always been and forever will be against the righteous; for we are his biggest threat; but not only are we Satan's biggest threat, but the body of the believers together is as well. Satan doesn't want unity to abide in church so he tries to creep in, finding himself a seat in the pulpit.

WITCHCRAFT IN THE CHURCH

It is time for the church to get in proper order to the divine will of God! We must know that everything that God does is done in divine order. From the very beginning of time order was very significant in the creation of the world. God created everything and everything that He created was created in an orderly fashion. Once God said let there be light, light was brought forth. And after God had completed His miraculous creation, He rested on the seventh day. God has all the authority over everyone and everything that is living and that is extinct. Even angels, God has all the authority over them. However, when God sends His angels out to do a specific assignment, they fulfill their assignment at that particular moment—at the right hour, on the right day, in the right week, and in the right year. Every work that God does is excellent, and since we are products of Him, we have to do things in a spirit of excellence.

The first thing that we need to do is get in proper order the divine will of God. Secondly, to fully understand order, we have to first seek out what is out of order. One way for a person to accurately understand order is by submission. How can we walk in divine order without submission? You and I must submit to our pastors and leaders of our church. We cannot think that we are too grown to listen to what our leaders are saying. Even if the pastor is a lot younger than we are, we must still be submissive to them. When we submit to our leaders, we are submitting to God.

The minute you say this is the church that God wants for me to be that is when you have made a proclamation that you are willing to submit to delegated authority. However, the minute some people join a church and after pressure arrives they then feel that they need to search for another church because they do not want to humble themselves to total authority.

In this life we must realize that everyone will have to submit to authority one way or another; and if we cannot submit to God or our pastors, how do you think that we will ever learn anything? *A leader only leads based on how well they have been taught and what they have been taught to lead.* You cannot do something that you have not been taught to do. The late Bob Dylan, a famous singer of our time, wrote a song that says "You Have to Serve Somebody" This song has a significant meaning to our life, which simply says, no matter who you are weather you are a president, governor, pastor or a leader you will still have to serve somebody.

KEEPING A TOTAL WATCH FOR THE ENEMY IN THE CHURCH

These are a few signs that a church can take to watch out for the enemy:

1. Unity

   If the devil can keep members in the church from coming together in unity he will slowly defeat them one member at a time; and if the church is not prayerful, the devil will then try to go for the pastor which is the head of the church. If the devil can get to the head, the whole body cannot function.

2. Prayer Base

   "Praying always with all prayer and supplication in the Spirit, and watch thereunto with all perseverance and supplication for all saints" (Ephesians 6:18). What is a major goal for Satan is to knock prayer completely out of the church. Satan wants the church to focus on other things that are less important; he wants the church to focus more on whose paying tithes, who's giving offering, which person has on the best clothing attire, who can shout the best, which person has the best singing ability. However if the church does not make prayer their first priority, it will not stand for very long. We need to bring prayer back to our church, because if prayer returns, revival will break forth, bodies will be healed, the dead will be raised, demons will be cast out, and lives will be changed. We have to stay active in prayer for our pastors, for our leaders, for our brothers, and for our sisters in the Lord. Someone has to stand up and bridge the gap, so it might as well be you!

3. Praise and Worship Life

The church must form a habit of praise in their ministry and in their everyday life. The more the church praises God, the more demons will be defeated. When you enter into the church parking lot, you have to enter in with thanksgiving in your hearts; when you enter into the doors of the church, the court, you have to go in with praise knowing that God is going to bless you. The devil wants to band praise and worship from the local church for he knows that in praise and worship deliverance will break forth on the scene. However, praise is a major weapon that every believer has to reinforce their authority over the enemy. In praise we can clap our hands, for in clapping our hands we can shatter the enemy. Also in praise we can stomp, march, and lift up our hands every time we are given the privilege to praise; we ought to praise! Satan wants every person to sit down on their praise. Satan knows that in praise each person receives strength—for the joy of the Lord is our strength" (Nehemiah 8:10, KJV).

4. Hatred is really big in many churches. This is why our praise and worship life must be consistent so that the enemy will not bring any division among the body. Many are experiencing drastic things not in the world but right in the church. Some people believe that they would do a whole lot better outside of the church than they would in. People are tired of the church fighting one another. The ones who are fighting are the leaders.

In the Scriptures, Jesus constantly speaks on love; he tells us that we are to love our neighbors as well as ourselves; and no matter who our neighbor might be, we are to love them the same way that we love ourselves. I found out the reason why many don't show love to others is because they find it very difficult to love themselves.

The church needs to stop *hating* and start *praying*! This is where we separate the church-folks from the Christians. A lot of church-folks will rather have someone to suffer than to help them, and not only are the church-folks doing this, but there are some pastors that will rather for their members to suffer and to stay in a box position rather than for them to push outside of the box and do a great work in ministry. Maybe you have experienced something like this before and you may have this as one of your questions.

WHAT ARE SIGNS TO LET ME KNOW THAT A PASTOR DOESN'T WANT ME TO BIRTH FORTH IN MY CALLING?

1. When you are not fully operating in your gift.
2. Not enough support from their leader. For an example, the pastor knows you are gifted and have a calling of God on your life, so they ignore your gift and allow your calling to abort.
3. Not enough tools. Not getting enough Word that will aid you for battle, instead they give you messages that will get you happy so that you will put more money in the tithe and offering basket.
4. Control: When the Pastor or leader tries to control you, instead of teaching what the Word of God says. A lot of the pastors who are highly controlling preach messages based on how they want you to live. This is a form of witchcraft, and I'm here to tell you that God is not pleased with this.

Out of everybody that is in the world today someone is being targeted by control, manipulation, and intimidation. As you have seen, these are a few signs that will give a person heads up to a manipulator, intimidator, or abuser in the church. However, if you are reading this book and you feel that you are a victim of abuse and manipulation in the church, you need to ask yourself, "Is this where I really need to be?"

You cannot receive the gifts that are in the promise land being stuck in the wilderness. It's time that you press beyond the wilderness and do what God has called you to do. Do not allow anyone but God to control what you say, what you do, or the way you live—for he is in complete control.

GET GOD'S APPROVAL ON THE MATTER!

If you need guidance in joining a church never join a church until you hear directly from the Lord. God will place you in the right church where you need to be, but you have to wait on his approval. Also, don't allow someone to pressure you to join their church when you know that that is not were God has led you to be a member of. You have the choice to say no! Do not allow anyone to control your thinking for you, but you think for yourself, because Jesus has set you free from intimidation, manipulation, and abuse!

FAMILIAR SPIRITS IN THE CHURCH

Earlier I have talked about familiar spirits, but now let me speak on familiar spirits that are trying to sneak their way into the local church.

Familiar spirits can travel through the church no matter the distance, and if the church is not in proper alignment to recognize the familiar spirits that are trying to creep in, the church will be completely torn apart. Familiar spirits do travel and they can travel a far distance to get to the place where they need to go; this is why a person goes from one abusive relationship right into another abuse relationship in another state, because a familiar spirit has followed them from state to state.

Take this for instance:

A family joins a specific church and the family starts to become active in ministry. The husband is a deacon of the church, the son is an usher, and the wife is the pastor's secretary. The family enjoys the ministry—enjoys the preaching, enjoys the music, and really loves the pastor; then out of nowhere, a female in the church catches the eyes of the husband, and later on, the husband and the woman with a lustful spirit began to see one another leaving the wife standing there clueless.

Months pass, then hatred and confusion begin to form. Now the relationship between the married couple begins to fall apart. So finally, the married couple and their children decide to make things better by moving their membership to another church.

And at the new church the family becomes active in ministry once again. This time the husband becomes the pastor's armor-bearer, the son becomes the leader of the praise team, and the wife becomes a Sunday school teacher.

Let's look at the pattern:

Yet again, a female that has a lustful spirit comes and attracts the husband's eye; this time, the demon is sitting doormat in the atmosphere waiting for the right time to allow these two individuals to meet. Later, these two exchange numbers and before you know it, under the sheets they go; yet again the wife stands there dumbfounded, when she finds out that her husband is cheating on her with another member of the church. The wife finally decides that she has had enough and can't take no more, so she leaves the church and makes the attempt to divorce her husband.

Before I go on any further, how could this situation be properly solved? Let me explain something to you: The enemy will follow a person for so long until they say enough is enough and enforce their authority over him. Familiar spirits in this case are very much similar. A lot of times a person wonders why every church that they attend, it seems as if the same routine is going on, this is not because of the church, but it is because of the familiar spirits that have followed that person to the church. But we have to break every evil pattern of the enemy. Every cycle of the enemy has to leave!

Do you question why things return back into your life? Do you wonder why you leave from one church completely out of order, right into another one even worse? You must realize that there is a pattern and confront it!

Let's go back to the family in the church:

The husband begs and pleads for his wife not to leave. He buys her flowers, a ring, and takes her out to dinner. After the husband has cried long enough, the wife decides to stay; but she tells her husband under one condition, "We are going to have to get some serious help if we are going to stay together!"

The family decides that they are ready to recognize the negative pattern, the familiar spirit, and put it to flight. This story would have all been settled if the family would have recognized the enemy when he first came in. A person cannot know a negative pattern is forming in their life and not being able to discern it without God first revealing it to them by his spirit. God will give us step by step instructions in walking into complete deliverance from familiar spirits and demonic encounters with devils. It's time that the church stands in the gap to pray, concerning the things the enemy is trying to form up in the church! It's time that we lay aside jealousy, envy, hatred, and strife! It's time that we come together as one—not trying to compete one person against the next, but for us believers to walk in total unity to the perfect and complete will of Jesus Christ. There is no little *I* and there is no little *U*, we can all work hand and hand in this.

BREAKING THE CURSE OF RELIGION AND TRADITION

True Christians are those who practice holiness away from the church. True Christians are those who practice holiness in the grocery store, on their job, in the mall, in the movies, and any other place that they go. But how is it that a person can show they are saved in the church, but when they get home it's a whole different ball game? We must lay aside religion, tradition, and every form of unrighteousness. This is the time that we walk in God for-real because there is no time for us to keep playing games with the devil. The devil is not our friend, he is our enemy; and if we continue to keep playing with him and straddling the fence we will be beat with his lies, schemes, and tricks every time.

"Once saved—always saved." This is a lie that has kept many individuals bound from receiving freedom into their life. But what some people feel is that being saved once is enough to cover their salvation for the rest of their entire lives.

Another thing that people love to use is this: "Well I have been baptized and that makes me saved!" Baptism is good and everybody should be baptized, but being baptized does not assure complete salvation. Doing the work of the Lord in obedience is what makes you saved. However, John in the Bible was a man that preached the message of God, whose objective was to baptize people, but John knew that someone else was coming who was going to baptize them with living water, with the Holy Ghost, and with power. John was paving the way for Jesus's arrival.

> They asked him, "What then? Are you Elijah?" And he said, "I am not." "Are you the Prophet?" And he answered, "No." Then they said to him, "Who are you, so that we may give an answer to those who sent us? What do you say about yourself?" He said, "I am a voice of one crying in the wilderness, 'Make straight the way of the Lord,' as Isaiah the prophet said." Now they had been sent from the Pharisees. They asked him, and said to him, "Why then are you baptizing, if you are not the Christ, nor Elijah, nor the Prophet?" John answered them saying, "I baptize in water, but among you stands One whom you do not know. It is He who comes after me, the thong of whose sandal I am not worthy to untie." These things took place in Bethany beyond the Jordan, where John was baptizing. The next day he saw Jesus coming to

> him and said, "Behold, the Lamb of God who takes away the sin of the world! This is He on behalf of whom I said, 'After me comes a Man who has a higher rank than I, for He existed before me.' I did not recognize Him, but so that He might be manifested to Israel, I came baptizing in water." John testified saying, "I have seen the Spirit descending as a dove out of heaven, and He remained upon Him. I did not recognize Him, but He who sent me to baptize in water said to me, 'He upon whom you see the Spirit descending and remaining upon Him, this is the One who baptizes in the Holy Spirit.' I myself have seen, and have testified that this is the Son of God."
>
> John 1:21–34 (NASV)

Baptism is good, but each one of us needs to be baptized with the Holy Ghost; for there is power in the Holy Ghost! The Holy Ghost will burn up everything that does not need to be; he will burn up religion, tradition, and every evil work of darkness.

BREAKING THE SILENCE OF THE FOUR WALLS OF RELIGION

> For the Son of Man came to seek and to save the lost.
>
> Luke 19:10 (KJV)

The objective in Jesus coming to the earth was to save every one. Jesus, God's only begotten Son, was on a mission to adopt others into his family; however, if you notice when Jesus began his walk in ministry he hung mostly around the sinners. Jesus preached and healed those who had a willing heart to receive; and their response was, "Jesus, Son of David, have mercy on me!" These were people just like us with real issues that needed to be solved.

I don't know about you, but I need for some things to get worked out, and I can't depend on the church-folks to work them out neither; but the only one who can work out my situation is Jesus. I can imagine the woman with the issue of blood being around a large crowd of church-folks. I can imagine some people pointing their nose up in the air saying, "she is sick to the point of death; don't let her touch you!" but not willing to help the lady in her condition.

The lady thought to herself, "The issue that I am dealing with no one can help me, but Jesus, He will be the one who will work out my situation."

Sometimes you will have to press your way through the crowd of the negative individuals, opinionates, and even the church-folk in order to touch someone who is the realest person that you will ever meet. Just touch Jesus one time and I guarantee you that you will not be disappointed. The reason why some individuals can't get to Jesus for themselves is because some church-folks are standing in the way.

DON'T BE THE
ONE TO JUDGE

Just because someone is not the way we want them to be does not mean that we judge them, needless to say, we are not the judge. A lot of the ones who are not saved have either been torn down by the church or have never had an encounter with Jesus for themselves. On a day to day basis I encounter many who have gone through a situation in their life in which they have been extremely beat down by the church. These individuals stopped going to church, because they were afraid that they might get beat-up or judged wrongly. But now is the time that we show the love of Christ to every individual, not just to the church people but the sinners, too.

It is not natural at all for you to go through cycles, after cycles of failure for the rest of your life. You must get to the root of the problem. Are you caught in the middle of abuse? Are you caught in the middle of manipulation? It is our duty to discern the person around us who is doing the abuse. It is not our duty to judge them but to show them love.

It is very imperative that we as believers use our discernment that God has given us. If you don't have the spirit of discernment and you will like to receive it, you can. Maybe you have been given the gift of discernment, but you want to receive more accuracy and clarity. Ask the Lord by seeking him in prayer and fasting, and he will give it to you.

The devil can't stand those with a spirit of discernment; he knows, once someone discerns his works by the Spirit, that person can send him completely to flight right before he makes his attack. The devil can detect when a person has been given a spirit of discernment. However, abusers in this case, seek out their prey by looking for weak individuals; many times if a person is strong, the abuser seeks elsewhere. We don't have to be vulnerable to the enemy through temptation or manipulation; for we are not weak but we are strong in the Lord.

How does Satan seduce a Christian? "Each person is tempted when he is lured and enticed by his own desire. Then desire when it has conceived gives birth to sin, and sin when it is fully grown, brings forth death" (James 1:14–15, ESV).

The Message Bible tells us: "Don't let anyone under pressure to give in to evil say, 'God is trying to trip me up.' God is impervious to evil, and puts evil in no one's way. The temptation to give in to evil comes from us and only us. We have no one to blame but the leering, seducing flare-up of our own lust. Lust gets pregnant, and has a baby: sin and gives birth to sin. Sin grows up to adulthood, and becomes a real killer."

Temptation comes to either make you stronger or weaker. Temptations also come to make you an overcomer or make you fall right back into the snares that Satan has set up for you. However, it is not a sin to be tempted; as a matter of fact, Jesus was tempted in the wilderness by the devil Matthew 4:11. It only becomes a sin when you do it. Each one of us has a decision to make, and the decision is either yes or no. Which will you choose?

Becoming a Christian does not mean that Satan will not come; as a matter of fact, Satan will come to try to persuade you that you can do a whole lot better being on his side. Some people get the meaning of Christianity totally wrong. Yes God will block the enemy from doing you any harm, but you have to know your battle strategies to defeat him. It is imperative that we use our weapons that come from the Word of God.

> So give yourselves completely to God. Stand against the devil, and the devil will run from you. Come near to God, and God will come near to you. You sinners clean sin out of your lives. You

who are trying to follow God and the world at
the same time, make your thinking pure.

James 4:7–8 (NCV)

Temptation and trials is a test of life. Each test is all
up to you if you are going to pass. As long as we are in
this world we will have many tests to accomplish, but
when we are being tested, it is our responsibility to pass
every test that is given to us. Your test might not be my
test; and my test might not be yours, but they are still
test that we all will have to complete.

> Then was Jesus led up of the spirit into the wilderness
> to be tempted of the devil. And when he had fasted
> forty days and forty nights, he was afterward an
> hungered. And when the tempter came to him, he
> said, If thou be the Son of God, command that these
> stones be made bread. But he answered and said, It
> is written, Man shall not live by bread alone, but by
> every word that proceeded out of the mouth of God.
> Then the devil taketh him up into the holy city, and
> setteth him on a pinnacle of the temple, And saith
> unto him, If thou be the Son of God, cast thyself
> down: for it is written, He shall give his angels charge
> concerning thee: and in their hands they shall bear
> thee up, lest at any time thou dash thy foot against a
> stone. Jesus said unto him, It is written again, Thou
> shalt not tempt the Lord thy God. Again, the devil
> taketh him up into an exceedingly high mountain,
> and sheweth him all the kingdoms of the world,
> and the glory of them; And saith unto him, All
> these things will I give thee, if thou wilt fall down
> and worship me. Then saith Jesus unto him, get thee

hence, Satan: for it is written, Thou shalt worship the Lord thy God, and him only shall thou serve. Then the devil leaveth him, and, behold, angels came and ministered unto him.

Matthew 4:1–11 (KJV)

We cannot be victims to the enemy; but rather, we must rebuke him and stand up against his seducing plots. When we pray against generational-curses, we must not just pray concerning the problem; but, we have to get to the root of the problem where it first began. One of the reasons why there are demons living in a person's family is because way down the family line someone who didn't put a stop to it was dealing with the same demon. However, you and I must make it our aim to cut off every pattern of the enemy, every generational curse. We must cut off every form of sin from of our lives. You do not have to live with a curse ever again! This is your day for freedom, because the curse stops here!

SATAN'S SCHEDULE
HAS BEEN CANCELLED!

> He that committeth sin is of the devil; for
> the devil sinneth from the beginning. For this
> purpose the Son of God was manifested, that
> He might destroy the works of the devil.
>
> 1 John 3:8, KJV

Now is your time to know that the schedule that Satan had on your life is completely destroyed! The hit out that Satan had for you is not only destroyed from your life, but it is never going to come back to hunt you ever again! Now that you know your place of authority, you know of your resources to use. You know how to defeat the enemy, and you know how his game plan works. Out of all the years that Satan has bothered you, he is going to have to pay for it all! Satan's works are going to pay off with fire and brimstone when God casts him into the lake of fire.

The thing that you must realize is that Satan does not have any place of authority, not now, not ever. The only place of authority that Satan has is what people allow him to have. Satan was never built to make people do anything; what he does is influence the mind, and the thoughts that he places in a person's mind it is up to them to go on with the plan.

Satan is not even in charge or hell, God is. God is in complete charge of both heaven and hell. If it was true that the devil was in charge of hell, don't you think that he can save himself from the flames of fire? "And the devil that deceived them was cast into the lake of fire" (Revelation 20:10). "I will bring thee to ashes upon the earth in the sight of all them that behold thee" (Ezekiel 28:18).

Many of you reading this book were on the devil's hit list, but because of the Blood and of Jesus being made manifested in the flesh, all of the devil's works were destroyed. The Bible speaks on Satan's defeat by giving us information to where he will be years from now. All of the lies, schemes, and tricks that he has ever used he will have to pay for them all really soon.

The purpose in hell is not to destroy God's children but its purpose is to destroy the devil, all sin, all sinners, and to make His righteous people safe forever. The Word of the Lord declares:

> God is good, a hiding place in tough times. He recognizes and welcomes anyone looking for

help, No matter how desperate the trouble. But cozy islands of escape He wipes right off the map. No one gets away from God. Why waste time conniving against GOD? He's putting an end to all such scheming. For troublemakers, no second chances. Like a pile of dry brush, Soaked in oil, they'll go up in flames.

Nahum 1:9 (Message)

You may be experiencing some pain right about now but God has a place far greater than where you are. God has a place of peace and rest from all pain, agony, frustration, sickness, and turmoil. Do you want to know where this place is? I'm talking about heaven.

Heaven is a place where only God's children will dwell; there will be no sin there, no flesh, no temptation, and no one to push the wrong button. However, Satan thinks that his attacks will save him from to tormenting flames of fire, but nothing he does will save him. Every attack that he brings ought to push you one step forward to your destiny, and also Satan's greatest weapons ought to push you closer to Jesus. There is something you must realize and that is, the moment you accepted Jesus in and told Satan no; from that point, you became Satan's enemy and he now has to do what he can to get you back.

Satan wants to be your god. He is not concerned with you singing on the praise team in a local church, but don't get delivered. Satan is not concerned about you fighting with a brother or a sister, but don't fight him. I found out that our biggest fight is not with our brother or our sister but with the devil whose job is to kill, steal, and destroy; but Jesus came to give us and abundance of life. As long as you are doing what the devil wants, you are alright with him, but what he doesn't tell you, is that, at the end of you doing his work there is destruction.

You and I can cancel every work of Satan by applying the blood of Jesus. In the Bible, the children of Israel applied blood to their door-post and because of them doing that they did not die. The schedule of the enemy can be cancelled through the Blood of Jesus. Apply the blood of Jesus over your life today! *You will never know how much power you have until you apply the blood of Jesus.*

No matter what it is that the enemy has told you or threatened you with, apply the blood of Jesus to that situation; for the blood of Jesus is powerful than any problem or sickness that you may have. The blood of Jesus is powerful than HIV/AIDS, cancer, sickle-cell, polio, diabetes, schizophrenia, bipolar, depression, oppression, tumors, arthritis, gout, limes disease, or whatever else the sickness might be. If you are dealing with a sickness, I decree and declare that by Jesus's stripes you are healed according to Isaiah 53:5! This is your day for healing! Rise up from your sick bed and be ye healed by the powerful blood of Jesus!

> For, behold, I create new heavens and a new earth: and the former shall not be remembered, nor come into mind.
>
> Isaiah 65:17 (KJV)

Behold, the tabernacle of God is with men, and
he will dwell with them, and they shall be His
people, and God himself shall be with them,
and be their God. And God shall wipe away all
tears from their eyes; and there shall be no more
death, neither sorrow, nor crying, neither shall
there be any more pain: for the former things
are passed away.

Revelation 21:3–4 (KJV)

Submit yourself therefore to God. Resist the
devil, and he will flee from you.

James 4:7

For Satan's work is cancelled from your life. No
longer will he take everything that you have, but this
is the hour that you proclaim that his schedule is
cancelled from your ministry, from your business, and
from your family. There are no more hindrances, no
more blockages, and no more delays; for today is your
set time to walk in the boldness of the Lord!

THE BEGINNING
OF GREATNESS

And I will make of thee a great nation, and I
will bless thee, and make thy name great; and
thou shalt be a blessing.

Genesis 12:2

The beginning of greatness begins with God and
ends with God—by him and through him were
all things made. There is nothing in this world that has
ever existed or that is living without God; for he is the
true reason that we are here today.

Every blessed day that we wake up entitles for us
to have a closer relationship with Jesus. Before we can
walk in the creations of greatness, we have to know the
creature of it.

The price that Jesus was willing to pay for us reveals great things for us in the future. All of the ridicule, agony, frustration, and the terribly bruised wounds that Jesus endured revealed how great we were going to become. At times we will be deceived, talked about, misused, and even abused but that reveals the crown that we will receive at the end. There is no pain that we are going through that Jesus didn't have to endure. If the world was against Jesus, wouldn't you think that they would dislike somebody close to him as well?

You cannot have the greatness of God until you remove all the filth around you. If you are filled with trash, God cannot give you an overflow because you are already filled-up with something else. This is the time that you remove all of the clutter from around you and fill your spirit-man with the Word of God. There has to be a total cleansing in order for God to create the best in you.

> And God said, Let us make man in our image, after our likeness: and let them have dominion over the fish of the sea, and over the fowl of the air, and over the cattle, and over all the earth, and over every creeping thing that creepeth upon the earth. So God created man in his own image, in the image of God created he him; male and female created he them.
>
> Genesis 1:26–27 (KJV)

This is when Adam and Eve messed up when God warned them not to eat from a certain tree called the tree of knowledge; but the fruit on the tree looked so great to their eyes. Adam and Eve were not good stewards over what God has given them, so they allowed Satan to move them from their place of authority. And when God saw that Adam and Eve were disobedient by listening to the lies of the serpent, He drove them out of the garden. This was a place where they could enjoy the wonders of the Lord.

Being a good steward does not only apply to Adam and Eve, but this applies to each and every one of us as well. However, God is requiring that we become good stewards over our money, time, business, and life.

> And God blessed them, and God said unto them, Be fruitful, and multiply, and replenish the earth, and subdue it: and have dominion over the fish of the sea, and over the fowl of the air, and over every living thing that moveth upon the earth.
>
> Genesis 1:28 (KJV)

God has given his children authority over the earth; however, some people use them having dominion wrong and try to manipulate others with the authority that was given to them. Some people feel that they can have any and everything they want without first having God's approval on the matter. Adam and Eve were just like this; God told them not to eat from the tree of knowledge, but Eve thought to herself "maybe one bite won't hurt!"

> From whence come wars and fighting among you? come they not hence, even of your lusts that war in your members? Ye lust, and have not:

ye kill, and desire to have, and cannot obtain; ye
fight and war, yet ye have not, because ye ask
not. Ye ask, and receive not, because ye ask a
miss, that ye may consume it upon your lusts.
Ye adulterers and adulteresses, know ye not
that the friendship of the world is enmity with
God? *Whosoever therefore will be a friend of the
world is the enemy of God.*

James 4:1–5 (KJV)

And the Lord God commanded the man,
saying, of every tree of the garden thou mayest
freely eat: But of the tree of the knowledge of
good and evil, thou shalt not eat of it: for in the
day that thou eatest thou shalt surely die.

Genesis 2:16–17 (KJV)

Now the serpent was more subtle than any beast
of the field which the Lord God had made. And
he said unto the woman, Yea, hath God said, Ye
shall not eat of every tree of the garden? And
the woman said unto the serpent, We may eat
of the fruit of the trees of the garden: But of the
tree which is in the midst of the garden, God
hath said, Ye shall not eat of it, neither shall
ye touch it, lest ye die. And the serpent said
unto the woman, Ye shall not surely die: For
God doth know that in the day ye eat thereof,
then your eyes shall be opened, and ye shall be
as gods, knowing good and evil. And when the
woman saw that the tree was good for food, and
that is was pleasant to the eyes, and a tree to

be desired to make one wise, she took of the
fruit thereof, and did eat, and gave also unto her
husband with her; and he did eat.

Genesis 3:1–6

If I was in Eve, instead of eating the forbidden fruit
like she did, I would have taken a big bite into the
serpent. You must understand that just because Adam
and Eve disobeyed and sinned against God, we don't
have to live under the curse of sin. Some people believe
that they are cursed because of the past generations
but those who think this way, are cursed because they
choose to be. However, Jesus died on the cross for us to
be free from the very curse of sin and death. Since Jesus
died on the cross for our sins, there is no excuse for us
to not live a life of freedom because we are no longer
bound to Satan. We now have the chance to be more
like Jesus. We must make it our aim to be like Jesus in
our walk, in our talk, in our thoughts, and even in the
way we live. For we serve a magnificent and great King,
and since we are connected to him, greatness lies in
each and every one of us.

There are three responsibilities we have in becoming
like Christ. First, we must let go of old attitudes.
Second, we must change our ways of thinking, and
lastly, we must place on the character of Christ by
aiming to become more like him.

> Till we all come in the unity of the faith, and
> of the knowledge of the Son of God, unto a
> perfect man, unto the measure of the stature of
> the fullness of Christ.

205

Ephesians 4:13 (KJV)

Beloved, now are we the sons of God, and it
doth not yet appear what we shall be: but we
know that, when he shall appear, we shall be
like him; for we shall see him as he is.

1 John 3:2 (KJV)

Becoming Christ like first begins with a decision—
you have to choose to follow Christ. It is your duty
to work your salvation and allow God to do the work
inside of you (Philippians 2:12–13).

Your first step after accepting Jesus into your life
will be to change your way of thinking, because your
thoughts become a painted portrait of your future; if
you want a life filled with abundance, think thoughts
that are good. Did you know that your life is shaped by
your thoughts? The way you think determines the way
you feel, and the way you feel has an influence on the
way you act.

With working your salvation you have to also work
the Word. Everything you need you'll find it in the
Word of God. You can change the course of your destiny
by staying in the Word. Meditate on God's Word, and
it will change what's wrong in your life to right. Think
on the promises of God and know that God's Word is
sharper and more powerful than any two-edged sword.
If you make your thinking based on the Word of God,
the blessings of the Lord will begin to attract to you.
What Are You Thinking About? Did you know that

what you think on will bring that thing into your life? Think successful thoughts.

God tells us in his Word that his ways are not our ways, neither are his thoughts the same as ours; this means that God's thoughts exceed what we think about. When doctors try to figure out how to save their patient's life, God has already worked the patient's sickness out before they even walked into the doctor office. I heard somebody say that *man's extremity is God's opportunity*.

When we have a problem in life that we cannot solve, it is our duty to think about the one who is the problem solver, Jesus and relax knowing that he is going to show up. However, the responsibility that we have in this life is to work the Word and allow the Word to work for us.

SPEAK LIFE!

Everything that is negative in our lives can all be changed by the words we say. We don't have to accept what the world says about us, but we can accept what God says about us. Everything that is in this world shall one day pass away but God's Word is the only thing that will not pass away—it shall stand forever.

You must hold on to what God has told you; for if he made you a promise he will surely bring it to pass. With working the Word and applying it to your life, you also have to apply the Word to your vocabulary. Instead of speaking negative words such as "I Can't", speak "I Can". Instead of speaking 'It will never work!' speak, "All things will work out for my good." You will be surprised to know how powerful one word can be.

When Jesus was tempted by the devil, he could have spoken a whole list of words to the enemy, but he only spoke a few—"It is written." That's all the words it took for the devil to leave; however, when we say words with negative meanings we produce negative things and people into our life. Also we must realize that when we speak negative words we give Satan legal access to do what he wants to do in our lives. At times people use the right words with the wrong meaning; and at times these people tell themselves, "I didn't say anything wrong!" while not knowing the meaning behind their words.

Have you ever told someone *I love you to death*? How about this, *She is truly beautiful just something to die for*! To the human mind these are just good words that we love to use, but in reality, they are words that produce negative things into a person's life.
Satan loves when we use negative words; sometimes Satan doesn't have to fight us but we fight ourselves with the words that come out of our mouth. Let this be the day that you decide to speak life! God created you for greatness, and since you have been created for greatness, your words must consist of great things.

When God created the world, he had you in mind. Out of all the eggs that were laid in your mother's womb, God still made the decision to choose you. The devil knew that Jesus was the Son of God from the very beginning. However, when Jesus was just a little boy it was in Satan's plan to have him killed. But God who knew what was about to occur, sent down his angel to warn Joseph to get his wife, Mary, and Baby Jesus to leave town.

If Satan tried to do this to Jesus, can you imagine what he is trying to do to us? The devil knows that greatness lies in each and every one of us, but we have to know it for ourselves. The minute we accept Jesus into our life is when greatness came. Greatness is a wonderful gift to have. With greatness, a person also receives the gifts of the Spirit. "Whoever does not know Jesus cannot receive the gifts that come from His Spirit; so this means, the only way for a person to receive the gifts of the Spirit is by having the Holy Ghost; for the Holy Ghost is our strength that will strengthen us in our daily walk in God" (1 Corinthians 2:14).

Every assignment that God gives, he always gives you the resources you need in order to accomplish it; however, God will not allow you to do something that you are not capable of doing. If God gives you an assignment to complete, the reason why he gave it to you in the first place is because he knows that there is more inside of you. What you think that you can't complete, God gives you the assignment showing that you can.

When you were born into this world, I can imagine God standing at the edge of the bed smiling at the wonderful soul that he had created. In the midst of you growing up, even in that time God was right there. God says in his Word that he has always been with you; he will never leave you nor forsake you; and even in your trials God is there (Isaiah 46:3–4).

We are products of God and were made to live a life of success; and the greatness that we have been given is all for the glory of God. God raised up teachers and preachers all for his glory. Long before he laid down earth's foundations, the book of Isaiah tells us that he had us in mind.

Greatness assures you that the promises God made to you are on the way. Some people don't quit have a clue to why they don't really like you and why you seem a little strange to them, but you are not strange, you are different. You are not just an ordinary person, you are extraordinary—you are a product of God. You cannot stop people from talking about you, but what you can do is remain at peace during the storm, because the same ones that spoke evil about you are going to need your help in the end. You are like a plant you need dirt to grow—more dirt means more growth. Some storms that you may have experienced in life God brought you out just in the nick of time, just to prove to the world that you can't live without him.

Though sometimes you are tried in the fire, God promises that you will come out as pure gold. The thing about gold is that when it is first dug from the ground it is worthless all until it goes through the fire. The first appearance of gold after it has been dug from the ground is a dirty black color; however, after it has been heated in the furnace for a little while it then reveals its great color. This goes to show us that while we are going through many persecutions God is molding and shaping us into the person that he is calling for us to be. However, being in the fire prepares you. Some of the most anointed men and women in the Bible had to go through many trials in life. God could have had the three Hebrew boys from being thrown into the fiery furnace, but God didn't stop any of it from happening (Daniel 3:16–27). God could have had Job set free from his many days of suffering, but he kept him in going through it (Job 1).

God allowed these problems to happen for these people to depend solely on him, and in them doing do so, they recovered all that they lost and a whole lot more. We sometimes have to go through the fire and experience a little bit of pain, then, after we have spent some time being in the fire, the fire will reveal who we really are—the fire will change our attitude and our demeanor. Sometimes painful situations will emerge but we are to still continue to serve God. For serving God, he has something good for us at the end.

> Nay but, o man, who art thou that repliest against God? Shall the thing formed say to him that formed it, Why hast thou made me thus? Hath not the potter power over the clay, of the same lump to make one vessel unto honour, and another unto dishonor?
>
> Romans 9:20–21

When a person sins they are no longer good for the Master's use; however when that person repents of their sins, they will have to go through another cleansing process. God places us in the fire not to hurt us but to burn up all the filth that is in our lives. Also, the fire prepares each and every one of us for ministry. The thing about a kindle is that it is used to make something that is worthless turn out to look great.

For example, the kindle is used to heat pottery. When I was in elementary, we learned in art class that when a clay structure is in the kindle the kindle has to be set at a certain temperature, or else the clay structure will come out deformed or broken; however, when the clay does not work successfully being in the kindle, it will ruin and will have to go through the process of reformation all over again.

From this day forward live your life in holiness being set apart for God; and remember, God is the potter and you are the clay. Don't lose your great appearance by running from the fire; don't allow sin to cause you to lose your shine. "Beloved, now are we the sons of God, and it doth not yet appear what we shall be: but we know that, when he shall appear, we shall be like him; for we shall see him as he is" (1 John 3:2 KJV).

Enjoying the Life God Gave You Being Free

Oh yes, you shaped me first inside, then out; you formed me in my mother's womb. I thank you, High God—you're breathtaking Body and soul, I am marvelously made! I worship in adoration— what a creation! You know me inside and out, you know every bone in my body; You know exactly how I was made, bit by bit, how I was sculpted from nothing into something. Like an open book, you watched me grow from conception to birth; all the stages of my life were spread out before you, The days of my life all prepared before I'd even lived one day.

Psalm 139:13–16, the Message

God has a marvelous plan for your life. The whole purpose in you being created was for you to enjoy life to the fullest. However, Jesus came as a prime example in showing you how you should live. Also, in the book of Ecclesiastes, God tells us that he wants for us to enjoy life, enjoy our family, enjoy the moments of our youth; however, in us enjoying life, God is requiring that we be holy in all that we do.

Jesus died a painful death just so that you and I can enjoy life in him. The moment Jesus said "it is finished" revealed the most secrets of life for the believers. On the other hand, the moment you told Jesus that you would live for him is when your new life began. For you are no longer living a life based on what people say or based on what people do but you are living a brand new life now based on the Word of God.

Jesus came to give you life to live more abundantly. Maybe you might feel that clubbing, smoking, and drinking is fun, but Jesus gives you something that will give you everlasting joy. Jesus made you for purpose. You do not have to do the works of Satan to fit in with the world. Jesus will accept you just as you are.

Maybe the devil has lied to you and told you that there was nothing that you were made for; the devil wants you to believe that you were just made to eat, to sleep, to get married, have children, and then die, but you were made for greatness. There is more to life than just what appears to be the usual. God has given you authority to live the life of your dreams, but only you can determine the way your life ends up.

The purpose of the believers is for us to have the ability to use everything that God has given us. God has a purpose and a plan for each one of our lives. "Do you know the plans that God has for you?" When you were placed into the world you were placed here to be a witness of God's glory. You were placed here to tell others the miraculous news that Jesus saves.

> Hearken unto me, O house of Jacob, and all the remnant of the house of Israel, which are born by me from the belly, which are carried from the womb: And even to your old age I am he; and even to hoar hairs will I carry you: I have made you, and I will bear; even I will carry, and I will deliver you.
>
> Isaiah 46:3–4 (KJV)

Psalm 139 lets you know that God will always be with you; for He sees and He knows everything; no one can hide from God. So since God sees and knows you, why not serve Him? Why do something sinful and get punished for it, when you can do something great and God will see it and bless you for it?

> From one man God made every nation of men, that they should inhabit the whole earth; and he determined the times set for them and the exact places where they should live.
>
> Acts 17:26 (NIV)

In times of us enjoying life to the fullest and completing a set goal, our main goal is to measure up to God's perfect plan. It is our duty to do the work of the Lord without murmuring and complaining. God is trying to get his people back to a place in him where we will make him first in everything that we do. If we can just return to true holiness as the Bible says, there will be an outpour of God's Spirit like never before; lives will be changed, bodies will be healed, and yokes will be destroyed.

This is your time to enjoy life, but will you allow God to be in the midst of the things that you enjoy? God has given each and every one of us family and friends to enjoy. God has given us wonderful places that we can go to remember that moment; however, nothing can fulfill our most heart's desire but Jesus alone.

Even though we may visit the most fascinating places in the world, no place will compare to our relationship with the Lord. No matter how much money a person has, they still will not be satisfied. The only one that can fulfill each person's desire is Jesus. Being a part of the family of Jesus is the best thing that can ever happen to you. One day Jesus is coming back for his people. Will you be one of them?

> And I saw a new heaven and a new earth: for the first heaven and the first earth were passed away; and there was no more sea. And I John saw the holy city, new Jerusalem, coming down from God out of heaven, prepared as a bride adorned for her husband. And I heard a great voice out of heaven saying, Behold, the tabernacle of God is with men, and he will dwell with them, and they shall be his people,

and God himself shall be with them, and be
their God.

Revelation 21:1–3 (KJV)

"Now that I'm saved, what do I do from here?" Now
that you are saved it is your duty to go and help save
somebody else. Show somebody else who is lost how
you found Jesus and lead them in that same direction;
but don't just stop there, tell everyone you meet the good
news of Jesus Christ and how they too can be saved.

> Even as I please all men in all things, not
> seeking mine own profit, but the profit of many,
> that they may be saved.

1 Corinthians 10:33 (KJV)

> But ye shall receive power, after that the Holy
> Ghost is come upon you; and ye shall be
> witnesses unto me both in Jerusalem, and in all
> Judaea, and in Samaria, and unto the uttermost
> parts of the earth.

Acts 1:8

> And Jesus came and spake unto them, saying,
> All power is given unto me in heaven and in
> earth. Go ye therefore, and teach all nations,
> baptizing them in the name of the Father, and
> of the Son, and of the Holy Ghost: Teaching
> them to observe all things whatsoever I have
> commanded you: and, lo, I am with you always,
> even unto the end of the world. Amen.

Matthew 28:18–20 (KJV)

In this Christian walk there is somebody that is waiting for you to come their way to bring them a word of encouragement, letting them know that they can make it. The whole purpose of the church is for each believer to work together in unity.

In the body of Christ one individual may be the leg, while another one may be the arm; each part is fitting in the body to do a work; if one part of the body was missing, the work will not be properly complete. There is no way that we can survive without the other; for I need you and you need me!

> For as we have many members in one body, and all members have not the same office: So we, being many, are one body in Christ, and everyone members one of another. Having then gifts differing according to the grace that is given to us, whether prophecy, let us prophesy according to the proportion of faith: Or ministry let us wait on our ministering: or he that teacheth, on teaching: Or he that exhorteth, on exhortation; he that giveth let him do it with simplicity; he that ruleth with diligence; he that sheweth mercy, with cheerfulness.
>
> Romans 12:4–8 (KJV)

God gave each and every one different gifts from one another, because he knew exactly how he was going to let allow his glory to be fulfilled in each one of us. I can imagine God saying "This child of mine really looks like he can sing, so let me place the gift of singing in him; this child of mine really looks like she can dance, so let me place the gift of dancing in her."

When God began his creation, he looked at you and me and saw exactly who we were going to be. And no matter what people say about us, God has already predestined us to live a life full of success. God looked at some individuals and said "Let me make them ministers of my Gospel; then he looked at some and said, "Let me make them pastors; then, he looked at others and said, "Let me make them apostles."

God has given each person a different ability for his purpose. If God made you a certain way, never underestimate the way you were created. If you are a singer, dancer, musician or a writer, just use the gift God gave you and he will perfect it. I, for one, have been given the gift to sing; however, it is my responsibility to excel in my singing. I found out in me practicing the more, my singing begins to get better and better the more I practice correctly; however in practicing, sometimes I found my singing a little out of tune, why was that? I was singing out of tune because I was not practicing correctly.

You must realize that when you practice something you cannot practice wrong and expect to perfect your gift, but practicing correctly will perfect your gift.

YOUR RESPONSIBILITY 'IS TO BE A LIGHT

If you are ever going to witness to somebody about Jesus make sure that you are living the life that you preach about. You cannot be a witness to someone if you yourself are not set free. However, before we can be a witness, "Let us test and examine our ways. Let us turn again in repentance to the Lord" (Lamentations 3:40, NLT), the King James Version says, "Let us search and try our ways, and turn again to the Lord."

The world is searching for someone that is real. Don't be afraid to tell someone the great news of what Jesus has done for you and how he delivered you. The sinners are not looking for you to come to them and tell them that they are in sin—sinners know that they are in sin, nor are they looking for you to come tell them about their sins, but what they are looking for is for you to show them how they can break free from their sins. Before you witness to the world make sure that you have the correct attitude and the correct motives.

Christians are a stage to the world and the world is the audience; in order for them get their audiences attention they must first decide to get their act together. Once a Christian makes a huge mistake, believe me when I tell you, the sinners will let them know. What a person does and the fruits that a person carries will show exactly how saved they really are as Matthew 7:16 tells us, "Ye shall know them by their fruits."

If you be a light to the world the world will follow you as you follow Christ, but can the world see Jesus in you? Won't you make the step of faith to get planted in the Word to produce more fruit; secondly, you can start by changing the way that you look at others. Stop judging others and examine your own attitudes, examine your temper, your motives, and your thoughts. Make sure that you have the right motives. This is the time that you enjoy the life God gave you being free; for you are no longer bound to the cares of this life! You are no longer bound to the chains of the enemy but you are set free to live a life full of abundance! God gave you this life, so enjoy it!

Do not walk around with your head hung down but

> Lift up your heads, O ye gates; and be ye lift up, ye everlasting doors; and the King of glory shall come in. Who is this King of glory? The Lord strong and mighty, the Lord mighty in battle. Lift up your heads, O ye gates; even lift them up, ye everlasting doors; and the King of glory shall come in.
>
> Psalm 24:7–9

So when you feel a little discouraged remember that Jesus loves you, and he is here to walk with you every step of the way, for the next step you take with Jesus is going to bring you another step closer into victory! The trial are only stepping stones to something magnificent. This is your day of total liberty! The king of Glory shall come in! Whatever situation that may have had you bound know when the king of Glory shows up, expect something great to occur!

CONCLUSION

Some of the many lies, tricks, and schemes of the enemy that God has given me, I thank him for the privilege in being able to share them with you. I honestly believe that if each person can get an image of Satan in their mind, they will be able to widely identify what it is that he's trying to do and place him right where he belongs—under our feet. Many have been beaten up by the devil, not because of the wrong things they have done, but because they have not used the right weapons to defeat him. Many have tried to fight the devil in their own strength, and after the fight came to an end, the person would always find themselves being beaten up by the devil. But this is the hour that we fight not by our own strenght or by our own power but by the Spirit of the Lord.

Each believer has a load of weapons that they can use to defeat the devil; but we have to practice in using every weapon that God has given us to the fullest. Remember, the fight is not with our brother nor with our sister, but with the devil. However, despite the many fights that we have to experience, we have the victory through our Lord and Savior, Jesus Christ.

This is the hour that we take nothing from the devil! In this season, God is about to upload witty ideas into the believers' minds for us to accomplish a great work. God is about to do a mighty work throughout the land. He is about to bless his children with miraculous things, but those who are ready and attentive to his voice are going to receive.

If you are reading this book and you do not know the Lord you do not want to live the rest of your life without him. You do not want to miss the great work that God is about to do!

The moment when I accepted Jesus into my life was the brand new start of my life. One thing I like about Jesus is that he is forever the same. Even though I have been saved for many years, I haven't always lived a holy life by doing what I should. However, there have been times when I found myself doing the wrong things when I should have been doing right; but despite of that, Jesus was still there with his arm wide open to receive me again.

When each one of us was born into the world, Jesus was still the same. When we began to take our first little steps, Jesus was still the same. When we are going through different changes in our body and hormones are starting to do their work, Jesus stays the same. When our hair turns gray and our bones become weak, Jesus remains the same.

The same Jesus that performed miracles over two-thousand years ago is still working miracles today. Jesus is still saving those who are lost; he is still saving the weary, he is still saving the brokenhearted. Many times we turn our back on God, but he is still there to receive us again because of his grace and mercy. However, God doesn't force himself on any man. Constantly Jesus is knocking at our hearts door desiring to come in.

In my weariest trials in life Jesus was always there. When it seemed as if no one was there to comfort me and when I was down to my lowest point, Jesus was there sweetly and peacefully whispering in my ear, "Get back up again My child."

Sometimes we fail to realize how bad it hurts when our arms are wide open to someone who are with us for a while, then out of nowhere, they turn their back and leave us standing there wondering why. Have you ever been hurt by someone who you thought was there for you, who you thought had your back, but in reality they left you in a time when you have least expected? Consider this person being you. At first you found Jesus and had a fresh zeal to learn more about him in the Word; you were determined to go to church every time the church doors flew open and you were fully determined to live a holy life; then, out of nowhere, trouble comes and the devil whispers in your ear that there is no hope, so you turn away from Jesus and follow after worldly pleasures. How do you think that makes Jesus feel?

Despite of your many failings Jesus is still the same loving Savior; and through it all, he is still standing there in the same place with his arms wide open to receive you again. Why not give Jesus an opportunity to live in your life? He wants to prove himself to you. Jesus wants to show you that he can be your healer, your deliverer, your peace, and your strength. Jesus wants to be your shield in the time of battle.

For one this book would not be complete without me giving you an opportunity to allow Jesus to live in your life. If you are not saved and you are reading this book, this is your day for salvation!

Maybe you might be saved but have not done exactly what God has called you to do in ministry, this day is for you! Jesus door is wide open for you to return back to him. Why not return back to your first love! Whatever you may be struggling with give it to Jesus; don't worry about what you have done and don't worry about what people have done to you; that is in the past; for it's time that you walk in the new! Jesus is here to restore you.

If you are sick and tired of the enemy playing games with your mind and are ready to be saved then say this prayer with me:

> Father God in the Mighty name of Jesus, I come bodily before You humbly as I know how asking that You will save me. Lord I know that You love me and sent your Son Jesus to die so that I might have life. Lord I know that I am a

sinner and I ask that You will forgive me of all of my sins. Lord, forgive me from every wrongful act, every wrongful motive, and every wrongful thought. Lord, deliver me from anything that I may be struggling with that is not of You; Lord, I now open myself up to divine deliverance for you to have your way in me. I accept Jesus into my life completely. Satan I renounce you and all of your evil ways, and I now make Jesus the Lord of my life. Lord I have just read this book and in me doing so I know that true deliverance comes from me confessing my faults to You; Lord I believe in Your Word, and I believe that you have just heard my prayer, and now Lord I thank You for forgiveness. In Your sweet and majestic name I seal these words and declarations believing it done in Jesus name I pray. Amen.

If you have just prayed this prayer the angels in heaven are now rejoicing. All of your sins have been erased, and you now have the privilege to talk to the Father for yourself!

Now that you have accepted Christ into your life it's like saying "*I do*" to Him at the altar and Him saying "*I do*" back to you just as what a man and a woman would say when they come together in marriage. However, once you say "I do" to God and acknowledging that Jesus is the Son of God you are simply saying nothing can separate me from the love of God; for the Bible declares that when a man finds a wife he finds a *Good thing*; however, the moment that you accepted Jesus into your life you not only found a good thing but you also found a *God thing*.

When two individuals unite together in marriage the wife will either move in with her husband or the husband will either move in with his wife. Maybe they both might want to start all over again and purchase a house together; however, when they decide what they are going to do they each will move their possessions in with them that they both had before they got married. What are you saying with all of this? I am simply saying that since you became married to God, the moment you accepted his Son Jesus into your life he now resides in you, and since you and him are now one, you have everything that you need. Since you have given Jesus the opportunity to live in you, you now have the privilege of receiving all that he has to offer. Healing belongs to you, his deliverance power belongs to you, the peace of his Spirit belongs to you, and the freedom of God belongs to you! Now all you have to do is receive Jesus, receive the wonderful things he has to offer, and accept it into your everyday life.

Some of the things that I have exposed about the enemy cannot compare to the many other things that need to be exposed. Now is the time for the true Saints of God to be loosed and set free from the yokes and chains of the enemy. The devil, has messed with God's children long enough, and it's now time for us to get revenge!

No longer will you walk around like you have lost everything but you will hold your head up and stand firm for you are armed and now ready to tare Satan's kingdom down. Satan has been exposed, his works have been destroyed, and you have been loosed to finish the work that God started in you to complete. This is your day to live in power! I decree and declare that as you have read this book your life is changing for the better. I decree and declare that this day you will gain more strength, more wisdom, and more knowledge to help you defeat every demonic force from out of your life. And Once again if you do not know the Lord, do not continue to live without him!

May the blessings of the Lord be upon you as you walk in your total breakthrough and dominion in Christ!

CPSIA information can be obtained at www.ICGtesting.com
Printed in the USA
LVOW04s2028060715

445141LV00030B/2117/P